The Nautilus Bodybuilding Book

Ellington Darden, Ph.D.

Photography by Scott LeG

Contemporary Books, Inc.
Chicago

Library of Congress Cataloging in Publication Data

Darden, Ellington, 1943–
    The Nautilus bodybuilding book.

    Bibliography: p.
    Includes index.
    1. Bodybuilding.   I. Title.
GV546.5.D37   1982   646.7'5   81-69629
ISBN 0-8092-5816-1   AACR2
ISBN 0-8092-5815-3 (pbk.)

Published by Contemporary Books, Inc.
180 North Michigan Avenue, Chicago, Illinois 60601
Manufactured in the United States of America
Library of Congress Catalog Card Number: 81-69629
International Standard Book Number: 0-8092-5816-1 (cloth)
                                    0-8092-5815-3 (paper)

Published simultaneously in Canada by
Beaverbooks, Ltd.
150 Lesmill Road
Don Mills, Ontario M3B 2T5
Canada

contents

foreword

I was introduced to Arthur Jones and his Nautilus training principles at the 1971 Mr. America contest. Casey Viator won the contest and I placed tenth. Casey and I were both 18 years of age at the time.

Two years later I visited Jones at his Nautilus headquarters in Lake Helen, Florida. Since then I've talked bodybuilding with him and his staff many times.

Arthur Jones is not a relaxing person to be with. He does not lightly exchange words. He spews facts, torrents of them, gleaned from his studies and, perhaps more important, from practical application of theory, personal observation, and incisive deduction.

You don't converse with Arthur Jones, you attend his lectures. He is opinionated, challenging, intense, and blunt. He knows more about the physiology of exercise than most people who are passing themselves off as physiologists in universities.

I happen to be in accord with many of Jones's ravings, and I find it easy to like him. But even if I found him repulsive, the contribution he has made to the realm of bodybuilding is of prime magnitude. Personally, I've used Nautilus principles and machines in my heavy-duty training for more than 10 years. It's worked for me—and it will work for you.

I've visited many gyms across the country, and I've talked with thousands of bodybuilders, including all the champions. Some understand the theory and principles built into the design of the Nautilus machines, and some don't. But all understand what they feel, and what they feel after Nautilus exercise is something they have never felt before.

You don't have to understand *why* Nautilus equipment works. But I urge you to try it; try it exactly according to the guidelines in this book. You may not understand then,

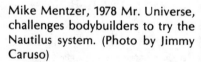

Mike Mentzer, 1978 Mr. Universe, challenges bodybuilders to try the Nautilus system. (Photo by Jimmy Caruso)

either, but that's not essential. Try the equipment with a tape measure in hand and see what happens.

Would it upset you to find that only four exercises—Nautilus multi-biceps curls immediately followed by negative chins and multi-triceps extensions immediately followed by negative dips—could pump your arms over an inch when the greatest pump you could ever muster in the past, even doing eight exercises for six sets, was a ⅝-inch girth increase?

Would you be unhappy if you trained for two years and then, after four workouts on Nautilus, found that you were able to add 15 pounds to your curl record and that your maximum military press poundage could now be handled for three reps?

If you work 40 hours a week and attend a university full

"The object of Nautilus equipment," notes Mike Mentzer, "is to enable the user to activate his muscles completely, intensely, severely, thoroughly, and quickly." (Photo by John Balik)

time and have only worked out for two 20-minute sessions a week for three weeks, would you settle for a 12-pound body weight increase?

The above examples are only some of what is happening to trainees I know who are using Nautilus equipment properly.

As could be expected, the Nautilus machines are being misused by some people. They do too many sets and reps and work out too many days per week. They don't understand or can't accept what a productive tool they have to work with. In essence, they're hitching a team of horses to an automobile and letting the animals pull the car.

Instead of rejoicing because there is now a quicker, more efficient way (notice I did not say easier) to achieve their goals, these people attempt to convert the equipment to what they think it should be. Rather, they should adapt themselves and their training to take advantage of what is before them.

The object of Nautilus equipment is to enable the user to activate muscles completely, intensely, severely, thoroughly, and quickly. It isn't easier, it's just finished sooner. Who works harder, the cross-country runner or the man who runs the 400-meter dash? Although that's debatable, it's easy to know who packs the most effort into the least time. By the way, sprinters are generally more muscular and powerful-appearing specimens than distance runners.

One young bodybuilder I know read about Nautilus principles and not only understood them but had the conviction to train according to the guidelines. He did one set of each of 12 different Nautilus machines to complete failure. When he began barbell training he weighed 139 pounds. Gradually his body weight increased to 163 and stayed there for seven months. After nine workouts on Nautilus it jumped to 178. He's growing before our eyes. His lats are thicker and wider; his entire torso and trunk are heavier and more muscular. His arms have gained $1\frac{1}{8}$ inches. And he's in very lean condition.

I've never seen a man correctly use the Nautilus compound leg machine who wasn't favorably impressed. No one, but no one, has tried Nautilus equipment and said, "Well, it doesn't seem like much to me," or any words to that effect.

Nautilus machines are not a fad; they will not just go away, like the hula hoop. I think they're more like the automobile. In the beginning, some people didn't comprehend the automobile's significance; even those who saw it, tried it, and approved of it, never thought it could completely replace the horse and buggy. In fact, it hasn't—not completely, anyway. I don't think Nautilus equipment will ever completely replace the barbell either.

Nautilus machines are not magical. The machines are good. They're better than good, but I know that not everyone who uses them will make the gains he should since not everyone will use the equipment properly. If you've been around free weights a long time and believe you know a lot about bodybuilding from reading muscle magazines, and then you try to apply barbell beliefs to your Nautilus training, you'll probably accomplish little, if anything.

But if you're smart and you study Arthur Jones's principles in The Nautilus Bodybuilding Book, by Dr. Ellington Darden, you and your training partners may be amazed by what happens to your muscular development in a very short time.

I met Ellington Darden, the author of this book, on my first visit to the Nautilus headquarters. He had competed in many bodybuilding contests during the 1960s and had just finished his Ph.D. in exercise science at Florida State University, so I was naturally interested in why he was working with Jones. Dr. Darden had met Jones a year before I did and had been studying and applying the Nautilus concepts for several years. He was convinced that Nautilus was the best way to train. We spent many hours discussing training concepts and muscle building.

Since 1973, Dr. Darden has written many books explaining Nautilus concepts. He has taken much of Arthur Jones's original thinking and made it available to many people in the sports and fitness world. It is ironic that the one group of athletes who can benefit from Nautilus equipment the most, the bodybuilders, probably understand it the least.

I know that it is difficult to accept ideas that are new, especially if they happen to challenge that which is near and dear to you. But remember—if you want to lead the orchestra, you have to turn your back on the crowd.

Mike Mentzer
Former Mr. America and Mr. Universe

THE DEVELOPMENT OF NAUTILUS CONCEPTS

1

introduction

The one subject on which most physiologists and physicians, trainers and coaches, athletes and fitness buffs generally agree is that Nautilus exercise machines represent the most important advance in the science of muscle development to happen in this century. Barbells were invented a half century earlier, and barbell-like machines emerged soon afterward. But comparing them with Nautilus equipment is like comparing an old Curtiss biplane with a modern spaceship. The Curtiss biplane got an individual to his destination slowly, uncomfortably, and unreliably. A 1982 rocket, utilizing every law of physics and electronics that we know, performs unerringly and transports a person through space almost instantly.

Arthur Jones, who invented, developed, and popularized the Nautilus machines, never dreamed in the beginning that he was establishing a new industry. He was a scientist, a thinker, and a world traveler, and he was interested in developing his own body to its maximum potential in as short a time as possible.

He was shocked when rehabilitation centers, veterans' hospitals, high school and university athletic departments, and fitness centers greeted with open arms his revolutionary ideas about muscle development. And when they began to buy his padded steel-and-chrome fabrications as they emerged from his shop, he suddenly found himself being treated as an honored prophet. Celebrities flocked to his exercise laboratory. The science of muscle building boomed and spurted to new levels of popularity and efficiency. Today, the movement continues unabated, with chains of Nautilus centers girdling the globe.

Yet, the logical muscle-building concepts of Arthur Jones have largely been ignored by an army of bodybuilders. This situation puzzles this man who embarked on his Nautilus odyssey in order to make self-training more scientific and effective for himself and others.

A JONES PARABLE

On occasion, Jones faces large audiences of athletes. With a typical group of bodybuilders, he is a tough, forceful, enthusiastic, and candid speaker. He never pulls punches. Knowing bodybuilders, and knowing their skepticism, he sometimes tells them a story designed to illuminate the importance of what they are missing.

"Imagine you are on a hiking trip in the middle of the desert," he says. "You see a figure in the distance. It is an old man, bearded and half naked, on hands and knees, with his fingers clawing at the sandy earth.

"You ask, 'What are you doing?'

" 'I'm digging for gold.'

" 'How long have you been at it?'

" 'Weeks—months maybe. It's awful slow work.'

"You notice the old man's bloody fingers, his raw and callused knuckles. You say, 'But listen, man! Digging with

Arthur Jones, inventor and developer of Nautilus exercise machines, is the president of Nautilus Sports/Medical Industries. (Drawing by Steve Rugg)

your bare hands is a pretty inefficient way to prospect for gold. That hole's only a couple of feet deep. Let me loan you my shovel.'

"You reach into your backpack, pull out a lightweight tempered-edge spade, and drive it into the ground. In less than five minutes you have demonstrated to the old fellow that he can make more progress in moments than he could in a month of using his bare hands.

"Then an amazing thing happens," Jones says. "That old man's eyes fill with hate and his face flushes angrily. He charges at you and grabs the shovel from your hands and throws it away."

That's the end of the story, and Jones's voice hardens with disappointment as he repeats, "He threw the shovel away."

The bodybuilders in his audience usually sit quietly for a long moment, digesting what they have heard, and then their lips tighten and their heads shake a little from side to side as they deny their guilt. But they understand. They understand that Jones is saying they are exactly like that old man in the desert.

Another speaker might have asserted that they were too dumb to appreciate the Nautilus way of "digging for gold." But not Arthur Jones. He made his point by talking about a dumb desert rat who, when offered a life-saving shovel (call it a Nautilus machine), became infuriated and threw it away.

Does his parable persuade veteran bodybuilders to abandon old routines and follow Jones's vision? Human nature, one hears, never changes. You learn a golf swing and use it for life. You fall in love with an old putter and you treasure it more than gold. Old bodybuilders don't change; they just pump away, doing the wrong things over and over. History says they will never change. Jones says, "I'm gonna keep trying."

THE NAUTILUS BULLETINS

Arthur Jones started trying to change bodybuilding concepts 14 years ago when he stumbled onto the basic scientific principles that led to his inventions. Hoping to persuade others to do their own experiments, he quickly wrote two documents, which he called *Bulletin No. 1* and *Bulletin No. 2*. Each was packed with trailblazing ideas. Each presented a breakthrough in human thought about the intricate cellular processes that continuously take place in the mixture of blood, lymph, nutrients, and chemical waste that bubbles beneath our skin.

What he wrote in those history-making bulletins is the foundation of all that will be written in this work. Maybe

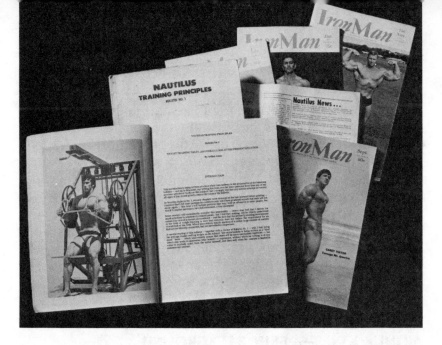

Arthur Jones's revolutionary training manuals, *Bulletin No. 1* and *Bulletin No. 2*, were published privately in 1970 and 1971. Copies were quickly purchased by enthusiastic bodybuilders, and supplies were exhausted in less than two years. Jones continued publishing his hard-hitting body-building advice in *Iron Man* magazine until 1974.

now is the time for every bodybuilder to gain, at long last, a proper understanding of what actually happens to his system during a set of 10 to 12 repetitions.

Each year, there is more to know. More knowledge is gained in science, math, and physiology every day. Times *have* changed. Life's pace *has* quickened. To keep up, man seeks a shortcut to every goal, and when he finds it he enshrines it and covets it.

Evangelists often talk about America's Great Awakening of the 19th century. Suddenly, millions of men and women "got religion," adopted a new value system, and practiced a different way of life. Perhaps this book can help stimulate a Great Physiological Awakening among America's young bodybuilders. They need no gurus to lead them, no cult to inspire them. The only requisite is common sense.

Each of Jones's bulletins made the same appeal years ago, when he insisted that the sport of bodybuilding would be improved by returning to basic logic and known physiological principles. There is little doubt that Socrates, Aristotle, Archimedes, and da Vinci used the same principles and methods that he advocated. Basic precepts never change. What changes is man's understanding—or misunderstanding—of them.

In this volume, ancient concepts will be repeated and amplified with special emphasis placed on certain variations such as pre-exhaustion and negative-only work. For the moment, however, consider the man himself, Arthur Jones of Nautilus, for a better appraisal of his intellectual and mechanical abilities.

ARTHUR JONES—A BRIEF BACKGROUND

First of all, understand that Arthur Jones is a man with a method. Rarely does he respond to a question by saying, "I don't know." Usually, he says, "Let's figure it out." On occasion, he uses a question to stimulate thought and to implant an idea. An interviewer once asked him, "How old are you?" His reply was typically Jonesian: "I'm old enough to realize it's impossible to change the thinking of fools," he said. "But I'm young and foolish enough to keep on trying."

The youngest son in a family of doctors, he grew up in a medical and scientific atmosphere. His father, mother, grandfather, uncle, and cousin were Oklahoma physicians. His brother and sister also became doctors. He spent much of his childhood reading medical books and applying what he read to the animals he caught in the fields and forests near Seminole, Oklahoma. From childhood, his interests were patently intellectual and the mental tests he took as he grew up invariably placed him at the genius level.

As an adult, his zest for life and his insatiable curiosity led him across many frontiers. For a while he operated a pioneering airline in South America. Later he built a booming business by capturing wild animals from wherever he could land an aircraft and then selling them to zoos and circuses. By 1965 he had become a leading producer of jungle and wildlife films. During this period he narrated, directed, and produced the internationally famous television series called *Wild Cargo*. He won his success through personal courage, by keeping his cool in desperate situations, and by forcing his inventive mind to produce solutions to mechanical and environmental problems that no other man had ever encountered.

Always, he sought to keep himself physically fit so he could follow a grueling work schedule more efficiently. When he had the time, he trained himself using old barbells and weights.

With Africa in political turmoil in 1968, Jones was advised to cancel movie productions until the dust settled. So he returned to America, to a village called Lake Helen, Florida, near Daytona Beach, and awaited word from agents concerning future movie projects. This forced vacation gave him time to exercise regularly for the first time in years. It also gave him time to focus his genius on the subject of body-building, a subject that had frustrated so many others who had built poorly constructed muscle-building machines in the past.

At first, as he did those curls and squats, he experienced a vague feeling of discontent. As months passed, he became convinced that performing a biceps curl with a barbell was so inefficient that it was ridiculous to continue doing them. When he studied other trainees he perceived the movement's essential awkwardness. So he began to imagine alternatives. Slowly, the elements of a better way—the Nautilus way—emerged. Throwing himself into self-devised exercise routines, Jones tested himself to the limit. His theories produced wonders of muscular development for him.

Reading, studying, researching, analyzing, and drawing fresh designs, he began to put together a machine that looked as if it had been created by a Martian. After testing it with battalions of volunteers, he could cite results of unprecedented efficiency and speed. No one would believe him.

Central Florida high schools are proud of their weightlifting teams. Jones took his theories to local schools, trained their lads, and saw those teams win multiple state championships. Suddenly he knew it was time to tell the world of his discovery.

Shifting from inventor to crusading scientist, he began to write. His articles appeared in a few magazines. He distributed pamphlets to anyone who would listen. Slowly, letters began to trickle into his laboratory from other dissatisfied bodybuilders. Some of them wanted to buy his machine or one like it.

He was not interested. Scientist Jones yearned only to deliver better health through a better body. He felt he had discovered a key that would unlock doors for millions, if only they would listen. His findings promised self-esteem and the prospect of vibrant health. Wasn't that enough?

The letters kept coming. Some contained checks, deposits on the first machines he would make. Others brought news from his agents saying that problems still existed in Africa.

"Okay, I'll build a few machines, and then we'll see," he told his friends.

In 1970 Jones established the research and manufacturing facility that would soon apply his theories to produce thousands of sleek training devices. Within the past decade his machines have been installed in every state and in more than 25 countries. He did not plan this. He did not dream of it. He merely did some original thinking, and things began to happen.

In particular, one of Jones's first trainees, an 18-year-old youth named Casey Viator, displayed unusual potential. Viator had successfully trained himself with barbells for several years before he met Jones. Jones convinced him to move to

The youngest man ever to win the Mr. America title was Casey Viator at age nineteen. This photograph of Viator was taken several weeks prior to the 1971 contest. (Photo by Inge Cook)

Florida and train under his supervision. Young Viator thrived on Jones's grueling workouts and made amazing progress. After two months of Jones's supervision, Casey Viator entered and won the title of Mr. USA. Nine months later, Viator captured the supreme prize of the bodybuilding game when he was chosen Mr. America of 1971.

All Jones had wanted was to convince the public that his theories were right. Most original thinkers exhibit the same determination: Thomas Edison demonstrated this when he performed hundreds of experiments before perfecting his electric light. And Guglielmo Marconi persisted until his wireless signal was the first to cross the Atlantic. And Henry Ford's Tin Lizzie was partly a vehicle for transportation, but mostly it was the embodiment of a concept for which the world, though unaware, was hungry.

THE NAUTILUS CHALLENGE

In the 1970s it became abundantly clear that the sport and science of bodybuilding had its own never-say-die personality.

His name—Arthur Jones.

His idea—a logical, scientific approach to muscle building.

His discovery—the fact that muscles are built best not by the volume of work but rather by the energy put momentarily into that work. In other words *less* work is better than *more*, provided it accords with the Nautilus principles.

A paradox? A riddle? A mystery? Hereafter are chapters devoted to explaining such matters and offering Arthur Jones's guidance to those bodybuilders who are willing to listen to scientific truths and common sense.

2

the power of common sense

The average bodybuilder wants one thing above all else: to build his body to its greatest potential. Currently, bodybuilders are attempting this by following the advice contained in muscle magazines.

Only a few reach their goal. The reason is that they are following inefficient and, in some cases, false training programs. In short, they are being misled.

Can such deception be avoided? The answer is *yes*. All a bodybuilder needs to do is to listen to his common sense.

In recent years hundreds of thousands of young men have adopted the sport of bodybuilding. Most of them, typical of our times, want instant results. The "now" culture insists that there must be a way to immediate success—press a button, get new strength from a jar of protein pills, or do a blitzing and bombing routine for the lats that will make the upper back look like that of a manta ray.

By the thousands, they train according to the directions in

slick magazines and paperbacks, as well as advice gleaned from bodybuilding workshops and seminars. But they get nowhere. They are missing a concept that Arthur Jones introduced to the bodybuilding world 12 years ago. He said it in five words: "Train less but work harder!"

The general belief is that the sport of bodybuilding has moved forward sensationally over the last few decades. Not so, says Arthur Jones. He maintains it has gone backward. He says this in the face of the statements in current muscle magazines and books that there are many more great bodybuilders alive today than at any time in the world's history.

Jones says the number of bodybuilding champions is not relevant. His argument is that out of every 100 enthusiasts, the law of averages states that there will be one man with above-average potential, 98 middle-of-the-road body-builders, and one dud. The reason we have more superstar bodybuilders today is that time has increased our sample at least tenfold. If we have 10 times as many bodybuilders in the world, we are bound to have 10 times as many super-stars. The result is nature's distribution method, not the result of better training.

What makes a bodybuilding champion among champions in the first place? Is it food, nutrition, training, or astrological sign? Jones says it is simply genetics. Champion bodybuilders come from a long line of large-muscled people. Primarily, they inherit their muscles from large, strong grandparents and parents. Without that kind of ancestry, without that heritage of potentially king-sized muscles, no one can be-come a champion bodybuilder.

Do the muscle magazines tell their readers that? Abso-lutely not! They want young bodybuilders to keep following their spurious recipes for success, drinking their protein cocktails, and eating their quick-grow energy bars. They lead trainees to think they can buy success—instantly!

How can dedicated bodybuilders protect themselves from irresponsible reporting or the pseudoscience advanced by some publishers? They can begin by understanding Jones's commonsensible formula of muscle building.

JONES'S FORMULA

In the simplest possible terms, here is Arthur Jones's argument.

1. The object is to build muscles.

2. A muscle grows only when it is stimulated.

3. A muscle can be fully stimulated when its fibers are rested and recovered from its previous workout. Hence, if the elements that compose recovery ability are to be available in the system, the body must be sufficiently rested.

4. Common sense prescribes that an ambitious bodybuilder must stimulate his muscle fibers at a stated intensity and with a certain regularity of rest intervals.

5. Thus, muscular growth is a result of *both* rest and work.

Jones's prescription is so logical that it seems every bodybuilder would apply the formula to his own workouts. But are bodybuilders concerned? The majority are *not*. Instead, most of them continue to train according to the formulas they have read in magazines, advanced by their favorite among the current crop of headlined bodybuilders. Like mice, most trainees follow their favorite Pied Piper to nowhere. Instead of thinking for themselves, they attempt to become carbon copies. Unfortunately, they copy the wrong people doing the wrong things.

A NATURAL MISTAKE

The current Mr. America, Mr. Universe, and Mr. Olympia winners were once unknowns. But now, they are pictured on glossy magazine covers, in advertisements, and on television. They are celebrities. So it seems natural that many young bodybuilders should be copying them, their training advice, and their routines. That's the way to become a champion, right? And rich, right? And be chased by beautiful girls, right?

Wrong! It is a mistake, though a natural mistake, to listen to most champion bodybuilders.

The muscle magazines make promises they cannot keep. Most physique stars deliver statements full of nonsense. When champions are asked how they succeeded, they name a dozen different routines, give pseudoscientific advice, recite their measurements before and after, their hours of work, and even the number of protein pills they consume. The truth is that they owe it to their parents and grandparents.

Though it has been said before, it is worth saying again: The champions owe their size to their genes. Their potential for big, championship, award-winning, gee-whiz muscles, came from some Hercules in their family tree, no matter what the magazines say.

No average man can ever develop the physique of a champion bodybuilder. His bloodlines do not supply the right genes to ticket him for stardom. But he can achieve many other important goals:

- He can vastly improve his muscular strength.
- He can increase his joint flexibility.
- He can improve the function of his heart and lungs.
- He can develop a positive self-image.
- He can become more proficient in almost any sport.
- He can augment his energy.
- He can recuperate faster than average from injury or illness.
- He can look and feel better by building his muscles to their maximum potential.

So don't make the mistake of imitating what most champion bodybuilders claim worked for them. And don't make the mistake of believing all that is printed in muscle magazines. Be your own person and use your common sense.

It is a mistake to listen to the training advice of most champion body-builders. "If you want to learn how to train a racehorse," says Jones emphatically, "do not ask a racehorse. If racehorses were trained as much as most bodybuilders train, you could safely bet your money on an out-of-condition turtle." (Photo by Dave Ponsonby)

TAKING A STAND

It is time for the leaders in the bodybuilding arena to take a stand, to throw out the bunk, to establish efficient training standards, and to level with the public about what makes a champion.

Nautilus Sports/Medical Industries believes that body-builders need and want accurate, scientific facts to guide their do-it-yourself sport. Clearly it is time for the Nautilus way to become widely known. This book should be read, digested, and applied by every bodybuilder who wants to reach his maximum potential as quickly as possible.

3

size or strength?

For years, exercise physiology textbooks have stated that "the strength of a muscle is in direct proportion to its size." Unfortunately, many bodybuilders have failed to understand this concept.

An examination of muscular size and strength, in simple terms, is in order.

1. To increase the strength of a muscle, a trainee must increase its size.

2. Increasing the size of a muscle will increase its strength.

3. If all other factors are known and allowed for, then a correct measurement of the size of a muscle will give an accurate indication of the strength of the muscle, and vice versa.

Once the above points are understood, the implications are obvious. Bodybuilders, who are primarily interested in muscular size, must train for maximum muscular strength in order to build maximum muscular size. Weightlifters, who are interested only in strength, must train for maximum muscular size in order to build maximum strength. In other words, bodybuilders and weightlifters should train in almost the same way.

UNRAVELING THE CONFUSION

Much of the size-versus-strength confusion comes from the habit of comparing one trainee with another. It should be understood that one trainee cannot be compared to another on any meaningful basis. Except in cases involving identical twins, it is scientifically impossible to make any sort of rational comparison between two men. Even in cases involving identical twins, there are still enough differences to make any comparison less than accurate.

This does not mean that a trainee must not make any comparisons. A truly meaningful comparison can be made by comparing a man to himself over a certain period of time.

ARNOLD AND FRANCO

Arnold Schwarzenegger probably has at least two times the muscular bulk of Franco Columbu. Yet Franco can lift more weight than Arnold. How can this be explained? Well, Franco certainly has more usable strength, but this is neither to his credit nor to Arnold's discredit. Rather, it is a simple accident—an accident of birth determined by heredity.

First, Arnold's forearms are much longer than Franco's. Thus, when Arnold curls a barbell, he must move the weight a much greater distance than Franco does when curling the same weight. Since Arnold's forearms are approximately three inches longer than Franco's, he must lift the weight six inches farther than does Franco. Thus, he is performing more work that Franco is, even though both men are lifting the same amount of weight. Therefore, the actual difference in usable strength is not always as great as the apparent difference.

Arnold Schwarzenegger (above) and Franco Columbu (below)—two of the world's greatest bodybuilders. (Photos by Inge Cook)

Second, Franco's attachment points may be more favorable than are Arnold's. If Franco's tendons are attached a greater distance away from the elbow joint than Arnold's are, he is also blessed with an advantage in leverage. Given this advantage, he could lift more weight even if his forearms were the same length as Arnold's, assuming that all the other related factors were equal.

Third, Franco's neuromuscular efficiency may be higher than is Arnold's. A cubic inch of Franco's biceps muscle may be capable of producing more power than an equal amount of muscle in Arnold's arms.

Fourth, the very size of Arnold's muscles puts him at a disadvantage. While it is true that doubling the size of Arnold's muscles will also double their strength potential, it does not follow that such an increase in muscular size will produce a proportionate increase in measurable strength. As the size of a muscle is increased, its angle of pull between the muscle and the tendon is unavoidably changed. In some cases, such changes will be to a man's advantage; but in most cases, they will be to his disadvantage. In other words, while the strength potential, or strength input, rises in proportion to an increase in muscular size, the measurable strength, or strength output, does not increase in proportion.

Because they fail to understand these points, most trainees are convinced that mucular size has little to do wth muscular strength. As a result, bodybuilders and weightlifters have drifted apart. In fact, the rift has become so wide that the styles of training practiced by bodybuilders have little in common with the training routines of weightlifters.

Someday this principle of size equaling strength will be understood and the information will be applied by many trainees. When that day comes weightlifting records that now appear unbreakable will be shattered. When a man who is blessed with a combination of all the favorable factors mentioned above trains to produce maximum muscular size, he will also be so strong that his strength feats will dwarf the best performances of today.

The best lifters of today are strong primarily because of favorable accidents of birth. In many cases, these advantages are so great that a man can lift enormous poundages with very little muscle mass. But what could the same man do if his muscular size had been developed to its maximum extent? This seldom happens because an individual blessed with such advantages is seldom aware that more muscle mass would make him even stronger. Furthermore, such a man is rarely pushed enough by his competitors to achieve his full potential.

THE BULKING UP MYTH

For years, most bodybuilders have made the mistake of bulking up—gaining size by adding fatty tissue. No amount of fatty tissue will increase muscular size. If training is conducted properly, any increase in size will be in the form of muscular tissue.

Apart from physique competition, there is little advantage in trying to maintain extremely well-defined muscles. But it is just as certain that even a small amount of unrequired fat is always a handicap. Paul Anderson is certainly strong; just as certainly, he would perform better with less fat. A person's car may operate with the trunk full of sand, but it will perform better without the sand.

NATURAL ADVANTAGES AND DISADVANTAGES

Many bodybuilders have claimed to have a 20-inch difference between their relaxed waist measurements and their normal chest measurements. But Arthur Jones has seen only one individual who actually had such a large differential: Sergio Oliva. Sergio himself admits that while this is an advantage in a physique contest, it is a disadvantage when it comes to Olympic weightlifting.

Before he ever thought of entering a physique contest, Sergio was an Olympic lifter—and a good one. He would have been a much better lifter if his waist had been larger.

Sergio Oliva has more than twenty inches of difference between his relaxed waist and chest measurements. While such a great difference gives Sergio a tremendous advantage in a physique contest, it is a disadvantage when it comes to performing overhead lifts, such as the clean and jerk. (Photo by Inge Cook)

This is not to say that it would be to Sergio's advantage to add fat to his waist. The heredity that gave him his proportionately small waist also prevents him from making use of the full strength of his legs and shoulders in competitive lifting.

Body proportions that are an advantage for physique competition may be a disadvantage for weightlifting, and vice versa. But it does not follow that bodybuilders and weightlifters should train differently.

Many leading bodybuilders will never be extremely strong, no matter how they train. Many leading weightlifters will never show much in the way of a physique by current bodybuilding standards, regardless of the way they train. But the same laws of basic physics apply with equal validity to bodybuilders and weightlifters—as well as to football players, swimmers, and participants in any other sport for which strength is important.

In the lighter weight classes in weightlifting, and in some other sports, it is not an advantage to build maximum muscular size—at least not in all the body parts. Eighteen-inch arms, for example, would not be an advantage to a sprinter—since they would contribute little to his usable strength in running and would add to the weight that he had to move. But increasing the size—and thus the strength—of muscles that are actively involved in a sport will always improve an athlete's performance.

CONTRASTING THE TRAINING STYLES OF WEIGHTLIFTERS AND BODYBUILDERS

Most weightlifters come much closer to training properly than do most bodybuilders. On the whole, few body-builders, Olympic lifters, or power lifters train properly. This is true primarily because they do not understand what factors are actually involved. Their opinions are based on hearsay or common belief. The fact that good results are apparently produced in some cases is merely proof of the productivity of systematic weight training rather than proof that a specific training technique was correct.

Current training practices used by weightlifters have two advantages over those used by bodybuilders: weightlifters usually train harder than bodybuilders and less frequently.

Unlike weightlifters, most bodybuilders train far too much and far too often, practicing too many exercises, and doing too many sets. But few bodybuilders train as *hard* as they should. While weightlifters tend to train much harder than bodybuilders, they still don't train hard enough.

Muscular definition is primarily determined by heredity and dietary considerations. If weightlifters watched their diet as closely as top bodybuilders do, and if they trained all of their major muscular structures in the same way they train for their lifting specialties, they would produce physiques much like those of bodybuilders. Furthermore, their physiques would have been produced by far less work than most bodybuilders devote to get the same results.

This does not imply that the current style of training used by weightlifters is correct—it isn't. But it is closer to being correct than the training style of most bodybuilders. At the very least, it is less wrong than the training of most current bodybuilders.

Unfortunately, weight trainees generally share a multitude of misconceptions and poor training habits. This is surprising, since many trainees are physicians, coaches, and physical educators who should at least understand basic physiology.

Generally, most Olympic weightlifters train harder and more briefly than do most bodybuilders. (Photo by Ellington Darden)

The physiques of some trainees are certainly outstanding, but they are the results of heredity to a far greater degree than they are the results of proper training. This is not meant to imply that champion bodybuilders are not products of their training—they are. No one just grew to such muscular size. But these individuals could have obtained the same results from a lot less training, in a much shorter period of time. Proper training would probably have given them even better final results.

IN VERY SIMPLE TERMS

In very simple terms, it takes muscle to lift weights. The more muscle a bodybuilder has, the more weight he can lift. Adding muscular size will *always* make a man stronger. Increasing his strength will *always* increase his muscle size.

4

the truth about barbells

The first adjustable plate-loading barbell was manufactured and sold in the United States in 1902. Compared to earlier bodybuilding tools such as sandbags, Indian clubs, and gymnastic bars, the barbell was almost a miracle machine. With proper use, a barbell was and still is capable of producing outstanding muscular size and strength. In fact, current bodybuilding champions credit the barbell with much of their muscular development. All in all, the barbell is an effective tool; however, it still leaves a great deal to be desired.

The basic limitations of a barbell are that it does not provide rotary resistance, variable resistance, or direct resistance. A reasonable knowledge of physics and human muscle function is necessary to understand these limitations.

The existence of a sticking point—the point during a barbell exercise at which the resistance feels heavier than it does at other points—makes it obvious that the muscles are being worked harder in some positions than in others. Likewise, when a bodybuilder locks out his arms or legs under a barbell in certain positions, supporting the weight without any significant muscular action, he should be aware that his muscles are not being worked in those positions.

Experienced bodybuilders are aware of both sticking points and their ability to lock out under the weight in some positions, but few understand the significance of them. Sticking points and lock-out ability result directly from trying to provide straight-line resistance against rotary movement.

ROTARY RESISTANCE

Muscular contraction occurs in a straight line, and straight-line force is produced. But the body parts that are moved by muscular contraction do not move in a straight line. Instead, they rotate around the axis of a joint.

You cannot proceed around a curve in the road by continuing to move in a straight line. In the human body, rotary resistance must be exerted against rotary movement in order to exercise the muscles in all positions.

Using Nautilus machines, which do provide rotary forms of resistance, a bodybuilder can produce a muscular pump several times greater than the maximum pump produced by any amount of barbell exercise. This fact proves that a higher percentage of the fibers contained in the working muscles are truly involved.

Pumping occurs because the working muscles require more circulation. If only part of a muscle is working, then only a small degree of pump will be produced. If the entire muscle is working, an enormous pump will occur from a very small amount of exercise. In fact, extremely lean individuals have been able to produce a degree of pumping that temporarily doubled the mass of the upper arms. After less than eight minutes of such exercise, the arms of these trainees swell to grotesque proportions.

With a fatter individual, a similar pump is produced. But it will not be so obvious because much of the mass of the arms will be fatty tissue. It has been noted, for example, that there is little difference between the measurement of a fat arm hanging in a relaxed position and the measurement of the same arm in a flexed position. A recent visitor to Nautilus Sports/Medical Industries had a relaxed upper arm measurement of 18⅛ inches and a flexed measurement of 18¼ inches—a difference of only ⅛ inch. When he asked Arthur Jones why there was such a small difference Arthur told him, "Because you can't flex fat." On the other hand, in 1978, Casey Viator, who was in very lean and muscular condition, had a difference of 2¼ inches between his relaxed and contracted biceps. Generally, the leaner the person, the greater the difference between the relaxed and contracted biceps measurements.

Now let's return to the pros and cons of barbells. When the pertinent laws of physics are understood, it becomes clear that barbell exercises tend to provide resistance for muscles only in their weakest or near weakest positions and that little or no resistance is provided in the muscles' strongest positions. Why a muscle responds by growing when exposed to high-intensity exercise is really of little importance, as long as you realize that it does respond this way. It should be obvious that growth stimulation cannot be induced if no resistance is imposed. And that is exactly what happens in most barbell exercises when the muscles are fully contracted.

VARIABLE RESISTANCE

In spite of the lack of rotary resistance in barbell exercises, they do provide a certain amount of variation in resistance. In some cases such variation is a decided advantage; in others it is a handicap. Sometimes both advantages and disadvantages are found in the same exercise. For example, in the barbell curl the effective resistance, or torque, increases as the movement progresses from the starting posi-

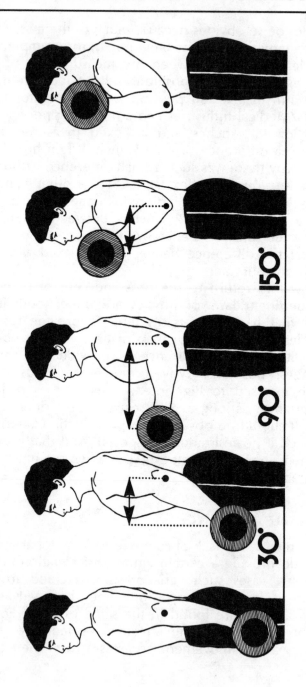

THE EFFECTIVE RESISTANCE IN A BARBELL CURL

To understand some of the problems behind exercises performed with barbells and dumbbells—for example, the barbell curl—bodybuilders should have a general understanding of two concepts: *horizontal distance* and *effective resistance.*

Horizontal distance is the length of the horizontal line between the center of the barbell and your axis of rotation. The elbow is the primary axis of rotation used in a standing curl. In physics, this horizontal distance is referred to as *moment arm or lever arm.*

Effective resistance is the rotational force that is exerted on a working muscle. It is determined by multiplying the horizontal distance by the weight of the barbell. Effective resistance is also called *torque.*

As a barbell curl is performed, the horizontal distance between the elbow and the center of the barbell changes. As this distance changes, the effective resistance exerted on the biceps muscles increases or decreases. The drawings illustrate the phases of a curl with a 100-pound barbell.

1. The horizontal distance between the elbows and the barbell is zero since most bodybuilders would move their elbows and shoulders slightly forward at the start of a curl. For all practical purposes, 100 pounds × 0 inches = 0 inch pounds of effective resistance.

2. At 30 degrees of elbow flexion, the horizontal distance is 6 inches. Thus, 100 pounds × 6 inches = 600 inch pounds of effective resistance.

3. At 90 degrees of flexion, the horizontal distance from the elbows to the center of the barbell is 12 inches. Thus, 100 pounds × 12 inches = 1,200 inch pounds of effective resistance.

4. At 150 degrees of elbow flexion, the horizontal distance is again 6 inches. Thus, 100 pounds × 6 inches = 600 inch pounds of effective resistance.

5. At the completion of a curl, most bodybuilders move their elbows forward to a position that lies directly under the center of the barbell. Thus, 100 pounds × 0 inches = 0 inch pounds of effective resistance.

As the horizontal distance changes in the barbell curl, the effective resistance increases and decreases symmetrically to and from a maximum at 90 degrees, or mid-flexion. Ideally, the effective resistance should be highest at approximately 140 degrees of flexion.

The effective resistance provided by the barbell curl does not match the potential strength curve of the biceps. The barbell curl, therefore, does not and cannot stimulate maximum growth of the involved muscles. (Drawing by Paul Hillman)

tion to the sticking point. But when the curl passes the sticking point, the torque rapidly decreases to zero. This variation of resistance is an advantage during the first part of the movement because the resistance is increasing at the same time as the available strength for producing the movement is increasing. After passing the sticking point, however, the resultant decrease in resistance is a decided disadvantage.

When Mr. America winner Boyer Coe first visited the Nautilus headquarters in 1970, he found himself very weak in the contracted position of the Nautilus biceps machine. Boyer, because of his experience in training with barbells, had become particularly strong in the mid-range of a curl. But since a barbell provides little resistance in the fully contracted position of an arm-curling movement, Boyer had never been taxed in this part of his biceps muscle. Many people who have trained with barbells note similar difficulty when they train on Nautilus equipment. Most barbell exercises do not provide appropriate variable resistance.

Because of the restricted ranges of movement and other factors, it is possible to perform a few barbell exercises so that the variations in resistance are entirely positive in nature, even if not perfect. In such cases a barbell is the tool of choice, primarily because of cost. The best of such exercises are wrist curls, calf raises, and stiff-legged deadlifts. These exercises should be performed so that the resistance increases throughout the movement. This technique will not result in the precisely correct rate of resistance increase, but it will at least be an improvement over most barbell exercises.

Muscles need increasing resistance as they contract because of the manner in which they function and because of their basic shape.

MUSCLE FUNCTION AND SHAPE

The all-or-nothing principle of muscular fiber action states that individual muscle fibers perform work by contracting (reducing their length) and that they are incapable of performing variable degrees of work. They are either working as hard as possible, or not at all. When a light movement is performed, for example, rather than requiring a slight effort on the part of many muscle fibers, the action involves only the exact number of fibers required to perform the movement, working to the limit of their immediate ability. The nonworking fibers in the muscle may be moved about by the movement, but they will contribute nothing to the work being performed. It should therefore be obvious that all the fibers in a muscle will be used only when they are all required to overcome the resistance.

In practice, this is difficult to achieve because all the available fibers cannot be involved unless the muscle is fully contracted. And it should be clear that the whole muscle can be fully contracted only when all the individual fibers are contracted at the same time. To perform work, individual fibers must grow shorter. If all the fibers are shortened at the same time, the whole muscle is fully contracted.

Still, achieving a position of full contraction does not always involve the working of all the fibers. Only the actual number of fibers required to meet a momentarily imposed load will be called into play. Thus, in order to involve 100% of the fibers in a particular movement, two conditions must be met: (1) The muscle and its related body part must be fully contracted. (2) A load must be imposed that is heavy enough to require the work of all of the available fibers.

In almost all barbell exercises, no resistance is encountered in the fully contracted position. In the top position of the barbell squat, for instance, when the front thighs are contracted, no resistance is imposed on the thigh muscles. In the finishing position of the curl, when the biceps muscles of the arms are fully contracted, there is little resistance. In the locked-out position of a bench press, when the triceps are fully contracted and the pectorals and deltoids are as close to being fully contracted as they will ever be, there is no resistance. Dozens of other exercises have the same fault.

When a muscle is exposed to *rotary* resistance it becomes

evident that the strength of the muscle increases as it is transformed from full stretch to full contraction. This indicates that more fibers are involved in the work when the muscle is fully contracted. At least, they are at work if resistance that requires their assistance is imposed.

Muscular structures are thickest in the middle, which indicates the presence of a greater number of muscle fibers in that area. Therefore, the midsection of the muscle is the last part to be called into play in a maximum effort. Furthermore, it stands to reason that this midsection cannot be called into play unless the whole muscle is fully contracted. So it seems that contraction starts at the ends and gradually moves inward toward the middle of the muscle.

DIRECT RESISTANCE

Most human movements are compound in nature. They involve rotation around two or more joints and employ several different muscle groups. Duplicating compound movements is another problem with barbells. If, for example, you try to exercise your upper torso muscles with a barbell, your arm muscles must also work. Since torso muscles are larger and stronger than arm muscles, the arms may fail at some point during the exercise before the torso muscles have reached their limit. Various forms of chinning movements, for example, provide a much higher order of work for the bending muscles of the upper arms than they do for the torso muscles. You can easily prove this to yourself. Perform four sets of regular chins, with a four-minute rest in between sets, carrying each set to the point of failure.

Forty-eight hours later, if you have worked as hard as possible, you will be so sore that you cannot fully straighten your arms. You'll feel this soreness almost entirely in your arms and very little in the torso muscles.

Pullovers with a barbell are another example. In bent-armed pullovers, you are limited to the weight that your tri-

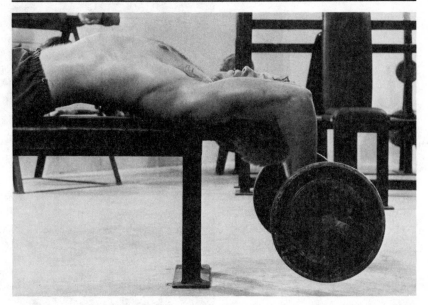

The bent-armed pullover with a barbell does *not* provide rotary or direct resistance for the latissimus dorsi muscles. You are always limited by the strength of your triceps.

ceps muscles can hold away from your head. In straight-armed pullovers, the strength of the elbow tendons is another limiting factor.

In both forms of pullovers, the limitations on range of movement are very much in evidence. Not more than 90 degrees of worthwhile rotary movement is possible, yet the upper arms that the latissimus dorsi muscles move have a total range of movement in excess of 240 degrees.

To work the torso muscles correctly, resistance must be applied directly to the body part that is actually attached to and moved by the torso. In practice, the resistance must be applied directly against the upper arms. What happens to the uninvolved forearms and hands during the exercise is not important.

It should be apparent by now that all barbell exercises for the torso and trunk muscles are limited because of a lack of direct resistance. When using barbells it is impossible to

In contrast to a barbell pullover, the Nautilus pullover machine places the resistance directly against the upper arms. In this machine it is possible to rotate the upper arms around the shoulders in excess of 240 degrees. The effective range of movement in a barbell pullover is less than 90 degrees. (Photo by Inge Cook)

provide full-range resistance or actually-heavy resistance for the torso and trunk muscles. Yet, in spite of these limiting factors, great degrees of improvement in the size and strength of these muscular structures can be produced by barbells—eventually.

In summary, the use of a barbell is limited by simple, unchangeable laws of physics. Barbells cannot provide the required rotary form of resistance. Full-range movements are impossible with a barbell in all but a few exercises. Barbells do not provide an automatically varying resistance that changes during the performance of each repetition. At best, barbells provide only limited amounts of direct resistance, and even these movements are restricted to the arms and the calves.

Finally, it should be understood that barbells can be productive when used properly. Again, compared to all earlier tools devised for physical improvement, the barbell remains a miracle machine.

5

the secrets of muscular action

I have yet to meet a bodybuilder who was aware of the prime function of the most commonly mentioned muscle in the body, the biceps of the upper arm.

—*Arthur Jones*

BICEPS

The prime action of the biceps is supination, or twisting of the hand. On the right arm, the biceps supinates the hand in a clockwise direction; on the left, the twisting is done counterclockwise. The bending action accomplished by the biceps is strictly secondary. One simple test will prove this: Bend the forearm toward the upper arm as far as possible, while keeping the hand in a pronated position. Place the other hand on the biceps of the bent arm. Note that the biceps is not contracted, even though the bending action has been completed. In other words, though the arm is bent as far as possible, the biceps has only performed part of its function. Now twist the hand of the bent arm into a supinated position and feel the biceps contract. Full contraction of the biceps results in twisting the hand and forearm, and the biceps cannot fully contract unless this twisting takes place.

For this reason, a bodybuilder can curl more in a normal, palms-up position than he can in a reverse, palms-down

35

position. In the reverse curl position, the biceps is prevented from twisting into full contraction; thus it is impossible to involve all the available muscle fibers in the work being performed.

The apparent difference in strength that is so obvious when the normal curl is compared to the reverse curl demonstrates the fact that twisting the forearm increases the bending strength of the arm. It is also true that bending the arm increases the twisting strength. This is illustrated when you twist a leverage bell in various positions. It will be apparent that you can exert a greater twisting force with a bent arm than you can with a straight arm.

In Chapter 4 it was noted that muscles increase their usable strength as they change their position from full stretch to full contraction. Now it should be clear that what determines strength is not as simple as it might seem. In the case of the biceps muscle, bending the arm increases bending strength, but it also increases twisting strength. Twisting the arm increases twisting strength *and* increases bending strength.

Arthur Jones frequently uses the previous description as an example of the difference between the actual functions of a muscle and the actions commonly accepted by body-

A parallel grip for behind neck pulldowns is incorporated into the Nautilus behind neck/torso arm machine.

builders. Jones follows up by asking bodybuilders, "How do you propose to exercise a muscle in the best possible manner if you are not aware of the function of that muscle?"

How Does Muscle Contract?

Human muscle is, somewhat surprisingly to the non-scientist, more than 70 percent water. Approximately 22 percent of muscle tissue is protein. Of this latter percentage, the majority is accounted for by millions of strands of both a thin protein called *actin* and a thick protein called *myosin*. Given the presence of calcium, magnesium, and two proteins called troponin and tropomyosin, these two filament proteins can contract and move the limbs with great force and velocity.

The fuel for muscular contraction is a chemical compound called adenosine triphosphate, or ATP. When one of the three phosphates is broken off ATP to form ADP, or adenosine diphosphate, energy is released into the muscular environment. When actin binds to myosin in the presence of calcium, the energy released from the ATP breakdown is used to pull the actin filaments along the myosin filaments. More specifically, a bridge forms between actin and myosin. Energy from ATP breakdown is used to shorten the actomyosin crossbridge, which shortens, or contracts, the muscle.

The contractile units within muscle are called *sarcomeres*. One long strand of many thousands of sarcomeres is called a *myofibril*. Many myofibrils bundled together form one *muscle fiber*. With the proper input from the nerovous system, innervated sarcomeres contract, and the muscle as a whole shortens.

This entire process was detailed and named the *sliding filament theory* more than twenty years ago by noted British physiologist, H. E. Huxley. Huxley has been internationally honored for his theory.

—Michael D. Wolf, Ph.D.

LATISSIMUS DORSI

Another misconception concerning muscle function involves the latissimus dorsi muscles. Most bodybuilders perform exercises for the latissimus muscles with a wide grip. The wide-hand spacing, they say, provides more stretch and a greater range of movement for these muscles. In fact, the wide grip actually *prevents* a full range of movement. Likewise, wide-grip chinning provides less stretch than would be afforded by a narrower grip.

Furthermore, all conventional forms of chinning and pulldown exercises for the latissimus dorsi muscles involve working the upper arm muscles. As noted earlier, the weakness of these muscles prevents you from working the torso muscles as hard as you should. This being true, why do most bodybuilders work their latissimus muscles with the arms in their weakest possible position? Again, the arms are strongest for bending when the hands are in a supinated position. Yet most bodybuilders work their latissimus dorsi muscles with their arms in opposite position. Turning the hands until they are fully supinated (palms up), significantly increases the bending strength of the arms. It is then possible to work the latissimus muscles much harder than would be possible with the hands pronated (palms down).

When the elbows are forced back in line with the shoulders, as is done in behind-neck chinning and pull-

Performing the biceps curl on a decline bench, or a Scott curling bench, is actually less productive than doing the regular standing barbell curl. The most difficult position of the decline curl is when the dumbbell is moving straight up. This position is shown above. After this so-called sticking point, the dumbbell moves more horizontally than vertically.

down exercises, the fully supinated position of the hands requires a parallel grip (palms facing one another). A bar with this parallel grip can be made in a welding shop for a few dollars, and its use will increase your results in behind-neck chinning and pulldown exercises. The hand grips should be parallel and spaced not more than 25 inches apart. The Nautilus torso-arm and multi-exercise machines are both equipped with parallel-grip movement arms and chinning bars.

THIGHS AND BUTTOCKS

A third example of misunderstood muscle action concerns the thighs and buttocks. These muscles are commonly exercised by applying resistance that is almost 90 degrees out of phase with the direction in which the body parts are being moved. In the squat, the weight presses down in line with the spinal column. Neither thigh nor buttock muscles, however, can exert force opposite the barbell squatting movement. Instead, the frontal thigh muscles thrust the lower legs forward, and the buttocks muscles move the torso in line with the thighs or the thighs in line with the torso.

In effect, the frontal thigh muscles require a leg extension for direct exercise. The buttocks muscles require a hip extension or torso extension for direct exercise.

FUNCTION DICTATES EXERCISE

A review of the previous examples indicates that most of the major muscular structures do not perform the actions that most bodybuilders think they do. So be sure to determine the actual function of a muscle before attempting to select an exercise with which to develop it. Following are some examples in review.

The biceps muscles bend and twist the arms, so exercises must be provided for both motions.

The latissimus muscles, as well as the pectorals and deltoids, move the upper arms. What happens to the hands and forearms is of no concern to the torso muscles. But if you must involve the arm muscles in torso exercises, as you must in conventional exercises, you should do so only with the arms in the strongest possible position.

In summary, always follow these rules:

1. Move the involved body part to be exercised into a position where the muscle that moves that member is in a position of full stretch.

2. Note the position of the body part.

3. Move the body part into a position that results in full contraction of the involved muscle.

4. Note again the body part's position.

5. Try to design an exercise or an exercise position that will provide resistance over as much as possible of the entire range of movement. If full-range resistance is impossible, as it will be in most barbell exercises, concentrate on providing the resistance in the contracted position.

The preceding paragraph should make it obvious that the declined curling bench represents a step in the wrong direction. Rather than producing an improvement over the regular barbell curl, it actually hinders the production of results. If the slant had been in the opposite direction, so that the upper arms were held in a position almost parallel with the floor, but with the biceps side of the arm held down instead of up, exercise would have been provided where it would have the greatest effect. Resistance would have been available in the strongest position of the arms instead of being limited to the weakest position of the arms.

A knowledge of the specific actions of the major muscles is a vital step toward efficient bodybuilding. Do not fall into the trap of doing exercise because you like it or avoiding exercises that are difficult. In general, the harder an exercise, the better the results. An efficient bodybuilder does not look for ways to make exercises easier. He looks for ways to make them harder and thus more effective.

6

direct resistance

The most efficient exercise discovered by man is that which provides direct resistance to a muscle's contraction.

Most barbell exercises are not direct in any sense of the word. Some barbell exercises are direct only at one point during a movement. A squat, for example, is not direct at any point during the movement. A curl is direct only at the sticking point.

In order to be direct as defined above, the resistance provided by an exercise must be directly opposed to the movement. In other words, it must be 180 degrees out of phase with the movement. If the exercise is direct or omni-directional, an inch of movement by the involved body part produces an inch of movement by the resisting object. In effect, any movement of the body part produces an equal movement of the resistance. If the resistance is provided by gravity, this means that body part movement must produce an equal measure of vertical movement by the resistance.

Although the barbell squat is certainly a productive exercise for the hips and thighs, it does not provide resistance directly against the body parts moved by these large muscles.

The reaction of the average bodybuilder to all of this may be, "So what?" If that is your response, you are missing an important point: the lack of direct resistance is one of the major shortcomings of barbell exercises.

So far we have discussd only one of two meanings of the term *direct* as it applies to exercise.

To be direct in the other sense, resistance must be applied against the body part that is directly moved by the involved muscles. For example, in a curl, the involved muscles are attached to, and directly move, the forearms. Thus, in a curl the resistance must be applied against the forearms. For all practical purposes this is the actual practice in the curl, since the hands are effectively an extension of the forearms. For totally direct resistance in a curl, however, the wrist joints would have to be fused in order to prevent any possible movement between the hands and forearms. In practice, because of the limited range of movement of the wrists, and because of the positioning of the related arc of this movement, no significant reduction in directness of resistance is produced by wrist movement. A curl, therefore, is a direct exercise, while a squat is not.

An example of a direct exercise in both senses of the term

is the movement performed on a leg extension machine. In this exercise the resistance is always directly opposed to the possible direction of movement and is applied directly against the prime body part. Most barbell exercises, however, provide no direct resistance. Some barbell exercises do provide direct resistance, but only during a small part of the movement. In addition, a few barbell exercises provide fairly direct resistance over a wide arc of movement.

THE PERFECT BARBELL EXERCISE

The wrist curl, if performed in the proper manner, is almost a perfect exercise. It provides full-range directness of resistance and even automatically varying resistance that comes close to being correct.

To begin with, the resistance in a wrist curl is applied directly to the prime body part, the hands. Second, the arc of movement is such that the resistance increases throughout the movement. If the angle of the forearms is proper, the resistance reaches its highest point just as the involved muscles reach their strongest position. Third, the geometry of the involved joints and muscular attachments is such that the strength curve progresses throughout the movement, steadily increasing as the muscles move from a position of full stretch to one of full contraction.

If a trainee can be taught to perform this exercise properly, nothing but a barbell is required for producing maximum results. While it would be possible to design and build a machine that would provide slightly better exercise for the forearm muscles, the degree of improvement would not be justified.

A similar situation exists with the calf muscles, which is amusing, because the forearms and the calves are two of the easiest parts of the body to develop and because the required exercises have been in existence for many years. Yet most bodybuilders are convinced that the calves and forearms are the most difficult body parts to develop.

For the best possible results, the barbell wrist curl should be performed as follows: (1) Grasp the barbell with a medium, palms-up grip. (2) Sit with the hips higher than the knees. (3) Place the elbows securely on the thighs and make certain the elbows are higher than the wrists. The forearms should be on a declined surface. (4) Lean forward with the upper body until the angle between the biceps and the forearms is less than 90 degrees. Keep this position throughout the movement. (5) Flex the wrists. (6) Pause in the contracted position. (7) Lower slowly and repeat. (8) Do not allow the fingers to unroll. Keep the barbell firmly in the palms of the hands.

One of the very best conventional exercise is the one-legged calf raise.

JONES'S SEARCH FOR DIRECT EXERCISE

The entire Nautilus system of training was a result of a search for direct exercises. Arthur Jones began by looking for a method that would provide direct exercise for the latissimus dorsi muscles of the back. It was obvious to him that all standard exercises for those muscles left a great deal to be desired. Chin-ups, pulldowns, behind-neck chins, pullovers, rowing exercises of a wide variety, and all other standard exercises for the latissimus dorsi certainly do provide some work for those muscles. But they all have one common fault: they all involve the muscles of the arms as well as the muscles of the back.

The latissimus dorsi muscles are attached to and move the upper arms. For direct exercise, the resistance must be applied against the upper arms. What happens to the forearms is of no importance. A criminal is hanged by suspending his weight from his head, thus imposing resistance on his neck. If he were hanged by his hair, the hair might pull out before any results were produced in the neck. A similar situation exists in barbell exercises for the latissimus muscles. Instead of applying the resistance directly against the prime body parts, the upper arms, such exercises apply resistance against the forearms. This creates a weak link. A bodybuilder fails in such an exercise when his arms fail, not when the latissimus muscles become exhausted.

So an individual is limited in such exercises by the existing strength of the upper arms. Being smaller and weaker than the latissimus muscles, the upper arm muscles fail long before the much larger latissimus muscles have been worked hard enough to induce maximum growth stimulation.

THE NAUTILUS EVOLUTION

Arthur Jones was aware of this problem more than 30 years ago, when he built a Nautilus-type pullover machine in a YMCA in Tulsa, Oklahoma. Since then, the scientists at Nautilus have gone through many intermediate steps in their attempts to provide direct exercises for the latissimus mus-

The bent-armed rowing motion with a barbell is a popular exercise for the latissimus dorsi muscles. Most bodybuilders make the mistake of performing it with an overhand, pronated grip. Simply switching to an underhand grip increases the effectiveness of the exercise by placing the biceps in a much stronger, supinated position.

cles. While Nautilus makes no claim that the present machines are perfect, they are, at least, so close to being perfect that no significant shortcomings remain. Additionally, Nautilus is aware of the shortcomings and realizes that they are the results of compromises imposed by mechanical limitations and physical laws. As an analogy, automobiles would be far safer, less expensive, and more efficient if they did not have doors and windows. But, in practice, a driver must be able to enter and exit an automobile, so he must have at least one door. For any sort of practical function, an automobile must provide some view of the outside. So it must have at least one window. In order to use a Nautilus pullover machine, an individual must be able to get into it with his elbows in the proper position. There must be a means of entry and exit, even though this construction slightly reduces the efficiency of the machine. A not-quite-perfect machine that can be used is certainly better than a perfect machine that cannot be used.

Some of Jones's earlier Nautilus machines were slightly more efficient than the current models, but they were three-man machines. It took the help of two other people to get into them. So Jones was forced to compromise, and has designed and built more than 40 different models of the pullover machine in an effort to perfect its function.

intensity: the threshold to results

Every muscle has an exercise threshold, a point below which no increase in strength will be produced. It might well be called the *threshold to results*. This threshold is related to the intensity of effort. Surprisingly, it has no relationship to the amount of exercise, except to the extent that intensity limits the amount of exercise you can do.

If the intensity of an exercise falls below this threshold, you can train for years with scant results. When the intensity is above a certain level, muscular size and strength are produced rapidly. Actually, it seems that the higher the intensity, the faster the size and strength increases will be produced.

INTENSITY DEFINED

Unfortunately, most bodybuilders have little idea of what is meant by the word *intensity*. Intensity is probably best defined as *percentage of momentary ability*. The key word in the definition is *momentary*. Maximum intensity simply means that you are producing as much muscular force as you are momentarily capable of doing.

MEASURING INTENSITY

It is possible to measure maximum intensity or, rather, to estimate your maximum intensity in terms of relative percentages. When you are doing all you can at a given moment, your level of intensity is 100%.

But how do you measure a level that is less than 100%? During almost all forms of exercise, the level of intensity is constantly changing, as this example shows: Starting your exercise, you are capable of lifting 500 pounds. But if you lift 500 pounds, you can perform only one repetition. Instead, you lift 400 pounds, which permits several repetitions. Thus, during the first repetition, you are required to produce only 400 pounds of force. At that moment, however, you could have produced 500 pounds, so the intensity level is 80%.

This first repetition did not produce a maximum level of intensity, but it did reduce your momentary strength. When you start the second repetition, your momentary level of strength may be only enough to lift 450 pounds. Again you are required to produce only enough force to lift 400 pounds, so the intensity of effort is still not 100%. But it is higher than it was during your first repetition; it has risen to 90%. The fact that you are using a higher percentage of your momentary strength will be apparent to you.

Again, your momentary strength level will be reduced, perhaps to a point at which you can produce only 400 pounds of force. Thus, your third repetition will result in your being required to produce 400 pounds of force in order to lift the weight, and that effort will use 100% of your momentary ability.

The only factor that changed during the three repetitions was the intensity. Everything else remained constant. The weight lifted was the same in all three repetitions, the distance of movement was the same, and the speed of movement was the same. The amount of work performed was also exactly the same during each repetition. The energy consumed, the heat produced, the oxygen required— everything remained constant except the level of intensity.

Being able to measure 100% intensity is important because it assures that given muscles are being stimulated to grow.

MOMENTARY MUSCULAR FAILURE

It should be evident that intensity is related neither to the amount of work nor to the production of power. Instead, intensity is a relative term. It is directly related to the percentage of momentary ability that you are actually using.

Arthur Jones believes that an intensity of effort of 100% will produce the fastest rate of strength increases. His opinion is based strictly on experience.

It is possible that a level of intensity somewhat below 100% may be all that is required for producing maximum strength increases. But even if you know that this is true, how can you measure it? How can you know that you are producing the correct level of intensity? Even if you know that a level of intensity of 90% will be as productive as a higher level, this information will be of no use. Because you cannot measure it, you cannot know if you are producing that level of intensity.

In effect, not knowing just where the threshold to results is to be found, you must always be sure that you are going high enough to reach it. The only way you can be sure of this is to go as high as possible, to the point of momentary muscular failure. Momentary muscular failure is the *only* point at which you can be sure of your level of intensity.

If you performed as many repetitions as possible, and if the last repetition was almost impossible, and if another repetition *is* impossible, then your level of intensity reached 100% during the final repetition, and you have stimulated the involved muscles as much as you can. Additional exercise on that day for the same muscles is not desirable.

If, instead, you stopped a few repetitions short of momentary muscular failure, you may have done nothing to stimulate muscular growth and strength increases.

OUTRIGHT HARD WORK

"Let's begin with the legs," said Arthur Jones to Casey Viator and Sergio Oliva. Sergio was visiting Florida and about to go through his first workout using Nautilus principles.

"Sergio," said Jones, "let Casey get several exercises ahead of you before starting."

Casey began by performing 25 nonstop repetitions on a leg press machine with 460 pounds. Immediately he was hustled from the leg press to the leg extension where he did 22 repetitions with 200 pounds.

By now Viator's heart rate was in excess of 220 beats per minute, he was breathing like a steam engine, and sweat was pouring from his body. But there was no time to rest.

Instantly, Jones raced Casey to the squat rack where a barbell was loaded with 400 pounds. Then, Viator ground out 17 continuous repetitions in the full squat.

"Okay, Sergio, you're up," said Jones, as Casey, unable to walk, slithered to the nearest hiding place.

Oliva reached the squat rack after 17 repetitions with 460 pounds in the leg press and 16 repetitions in the leg extension with 200 pounds. When Sergio "broke the lock" in his knees for the squat with 400 pounds, he went to the floor like he had been knocked in the head. After being helped to his feet, he tried it again—with the same results. One hundred pounds were removed from the bar, during which delay Sergio was afforded some rest, and then he performed seven repetitions wih 300 pounds.

Sergio was accustomed to training his legs for at least one hour almost nonstop in the traditional fashion. But during his leg workout under Jones's supervision, one cycle of three exercises performed until momentary muscular exhaustion within a period of five minutes was all he wanted. Furthermore, Sergio spent a considerably longer period of time stretched out in front of the gym.

When Sergio recovered sufficiently to continue his workout, the torso cycle and the arm cycle were completed in approximately 12 minutes. Previously, his torso and arm training had taken two hours or longer to complete.

But, obviously, Sergio Oliva had never trained with the intensity that he experienced with Jones and Viator.

Arnold Schwarzenegger also went through a similar training session under Jones's watchful eye and remarked, "I've often experienced times during a workout where I had difficulty walking. But this is the first time that I've ever had difficulty lying down."

"Have you ever vomited as a result of doing one set of curls?" asks Arthur Jones to a group of bodybuilders, "If not, then you simply don't know what hard work is. There is only one way to the top in bodybuilding and that one way involves *outright hard work.*"

LOOKING BACK AT INTENSITY

More than 100 years ago people interested in bodybuilding performed thousands of repetitions of calisthenics with little in the way of strength increases. Their intensity of effort was far too low. Later, better results were produced through the use of Indian clubs, which reduced the amount of exercise but increased the intensity. In the early 1900s even better results were produced by barbells, and again the amount of exercise was reduced. Because barbells were heavier and provided greater resistance, it appeared that the resultant improvements were the consequence of increased resistance. That appearance was misleading.

Physiologists know today that increased resistance is a prerequisite to muscular growth, but it is not the catalyst or the trigger that makes growth happen. Instead, increased resistance makes it possible to work at a higher level of intensity, and this elevated intensity is the factor that actually improves the results.

During calisthenics, when no added resistance is available, it is possible to perform thousands of repetitions of some exercises. As a result, these exercises are normally terminated short of the point of muscular failure. The added resistance of Indian clubs makes the situation somewhat better. It is no longer possible for the trainee to perform as many repetitions as he could during unweighted calisthenics. Thus, he is more likely to approach the point of muscular failure. Though the number of possible repetitions is still too high, the increased level of intensity will improve the production of results. With an adjustable barbell, if the weight is selected properly, the increase in available resistance makes it impossible to perform more than a few repetitions. The same is true of Nautilus machines.

How Does Muscle Grow?

The technical term for muscular growth is *hypertrophy*. Its inverse, called *atrophy*, refers to the breakdown of muscle tissue from disuse. The process of atrophy involves metabolic breakdown of muscle into its constituent compounds, which are removed by the bloodstream. Atrophied muscle does *not* turn into fat.

Hypertrophy, or muscular growth, occurs as a result of demands placed on the muscle. The signal for hypertrophy is clearly *intensity of contraction*. When a muscle is faced with high-intensity requirements, it responds with a protective increase in muscular size and strength.

A number of changes associated with hypertrophy explain increased muscular size and strength:

- The actin and particularly the myosin protein filaments increase in size.
- The number of myofibrils increases.

- The number of blood capillaries within the fiber may increase.
- The amount of connective tissue within the muscle may increase.
- The number of muscle fibers may increase.

There is scientific debate over the occurrence of this last phenomenon, which is called *hyperplasia*. While a small number of studies on rats and cats has shown fiber splitting with increased muscular size, most researchers have not been able to demonstrate it. As of 1981, there is no evidence that the number of muscle fibers increases in humans when muscular size and strength is increased through weight training.

—Michael D. Wolf, Ph.D.

INTENSITY AND AMOUNT OF EXERCISE

Whenever any exercise makes it possible to reach momentary muscular failure, it becomes necessary to reduce the amount of exercise you engage in. When you increase the intensity of exercise, it follows that you *must* reduce the amount of exercise. A widespread failure to understand this point has kept many bodybuilders from reaching their full

Common laborers often perform enormous *amounts* of work. But in order to perform a large amount of work, their intensity must be kept at a low level. There is no such thing as long, hard work. Hard work must be brief!

potential. And many others have spent years to get results that could have been produced in months. Growth of muscular mass, and thus an increase in strength, is stimulated by high-intensity work. This work makes demands on the recovery ability of the body that cannot easily be met. So the amount of high-intensity work must be limited.

Failing to understand this relationship, most bodybuilders are tempted to do more than is required. The result is a waste of time and energy. Indeed, it is usually a total lack of improvement.

To repeat, you can perform a large amount of work or high-intensity work, but you cannot do both. If you insist on increasing the amount of exercise you do, you must reduce its intensity. You really have no choice in the matter.

8

why exercise increases strength

Exercise increases strength by creating a need for growth. It makes demands on the body that cannot easily be met by its existing muscular development. If the existing level of strength is adequate for the normal work loads encountered, there is no need for growth. The body will not provide something that is not required, at least not in the way of muscular size and strength.

Within broad limits, you can do almost anything you want to with a program of proper exercise. The limits of muscular growth are determined by individual potential. But within those limits, striking degrees of physical improvement can be produced in almost anybody.

Producing these improvements does not take years of steady training, nor does it require you to spend your entire life in a gym. Quite the contrary is true. Gratifying results can come very quickly from brief and infrequent workouts, while continuing other types of physical activity, and while improving your strength and stamina.

OVERTRAINING

Exercise should constantly improve your strength as you perform your exercises and simultaneously increase your overall ability in other physical activities. What frequently happens in practice is a far cry from what should have happened. Instead of producing an ever-increasing feeling of strength and well-being, an improper exercise program will leave you feeling constantly tired, with little energy for anything else.

A persistent tired feeling should be a warning that something is wrong. Unfortunately, it is a warning that is frequently ignored. If you are untrained, you will feel tired as a result of your first few workouts, but this feeling should not continue. If it does, you are overtraining. In short, your workouts are exceeding the recovery ability of your system.

On the other hand, as a bodybuilder, you should be tired at the end of a workout. This is true even though you may have trained for years. But you should not remain tired. Within 20 minutes you should have recovered and feel capable of going through your entire workout again. And you should be able to do so, even though you should never try. It takes very little high-intensity exercise to stimulate growth.

THE DEMANDS OF HIGH-INTENSITY EXERCISE

Somehow, high-intensity exercise is dramatically different from low-intensity exercise. Physiologists still do not understand the entire difference. What we do know is that high-intensity exercise makes demands on the body that are not quickly met.

When a muscle is working close to its limit, a change in body chemistry seems to occur. You do not need to know just how this happens. You need to understand that it *does* happen. Apparently, demands are made on the system that are never experienced during low-intensity work. If these

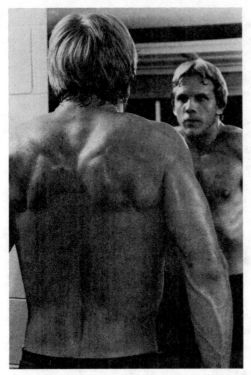

As the trainee shown performs heavy shoulder shrugs with dumb-bells, his heart rate, blood pressure, and body temperature increase dramatically. If the exercise is carried to momentary muscular failure, a change in body chemistry seems to occur that causes the involved muscles to become larger and stronger.

demands are ignored, muscle growth becomes impossible.

Consider a muscle that is being worked very hard. That muscle needs unprecedented amounts of oxygen and nutrition, as well as a purging of combustion debris. The support system of the body must strain to meet these outside requirements. At the end of a bout of exercise, that muscle must be given time to regain its normal state. If high-intensity work is again attempted before recovery is complete, a sickly muscle must result, with the unwanted accompaniment of losses in both muscular strength and mass.

By failing to understand this process, many bodybuilders have overtrained and denied themselves the benefits that a little knowledge would have assured. In their ignorance, many have attempted to avoid overtraining by reducing the

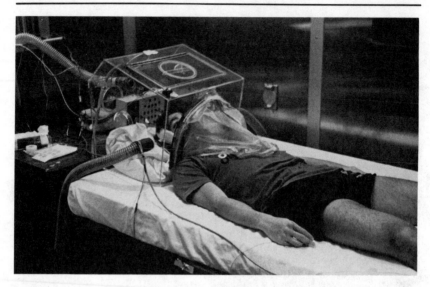

High-intensity exercise stimulates muscles to grow. But the stimulated muscles actually grow when the body is resting. Metabolic studies show that such growth takes place within a five- to ten-minute time period approximately thirty to forty hours after the stimulation occurs. (Photo by Ellington Darden)

intensity of their exercises, with the result that their muscle growth is no longer stimulated.

In either case, growth will not occur. Growth cannot occur if the body is overtrained and will not occur if the intensity of work is too low.

PERMITTING GROWTH

While exercise is capable of producing enormous increases in musular mass and strength, it apparently does not produce a proportionate increase in the capability of the support system of the body.

In practice, this means that a stronger man literally cannot stand as much high-intensity work as a weaker man. When regular training is started, a beginner will grow rapidly as a result of high-intensity training, even if he trains three or four times as much as is required. Apparently, a weak individual is unable to exceed the recovery ability of his system; he is not strong enough to impose a demand on his recovery ability that cannot be met. As he becomes stronger as a result of training, however, he starts making demands on his recovery ability that are difficult to meet. Now, his ability to make such demands is increasing more rapidly than his ability to meet them. Eventually, when a level of greater-than-average strength has been achieved, he becomes capable of making demands that simply cannot be met. At this strength level, the amount of training must be reduced.

Such demands on the overall recovery ability are related directly to the intensity of exercise. They have little relation to the amount of exercise.

If the implications stated above are understood, it is possible to produce good results from exercise. Without such an understanding, the best results are inaccessible.

CONSTANT RESULTS

How are good results defined? Unfortunately, *good results from exercise* is a relative term, and far too many factors are involved to permit a simple definition. Good results for one person might be very poor results for another. A body-builder, at least, can recognize constant results and he should be aware that *no results* does not equate with *good results*. Thus, a lack of progress is a clear warning that something is wrong. Yet thousands of bodybuilders train for years with little in the way of results to show for their efforts. That is certainly a satisfactory state if training is being conducted for the purpose of maintaining an existing level of strength. But that is seldom the case. Instead, the majority of such trainees are desperately trying to increase their strength, and they are failing.

For the production of best results, exercise must *stimulate* growth and *permit* growth.

9

stimulating growth

An experienced observer at any major physique contest will notice an interesting characteristic among the contestants: in almost all cases, the left arm of a right-handed bodybuilder is larger than his right arm, usually to a marked degree. This is true because the left arm of a right-handed man must work harder to perform its share of an equally divided work load. The left arm does not work more, nor differently—it works harder, with a greater intensity of effort. And it responds by growing larger than the right arm.

A right-handed man lacks some degree of coordination in his left arm. His balance and muscular control are both less efficient in his left arm. This remains true to some degree regardless of the length of time that he has been training both arms identically. Therefore, the left arm works harder, and its response to this increased intensity of effort is to grow. Research shows that in tests of strength that do not involve balance or muscular coordination, the left arm is almost always stronger as well as larger.

When Arthur Jones brings this to the attention of bodybuilders seeking his help, their response usually is: "Well, in that case, I'll do an extra set of curls with my right arm. Then it will grow larger, too."

MORE IS *NOT* BETTER

In order to achieve growth, most bodybuilders assume that more exercise is required when, in fact, only *harder* exercise is needed.

Lacking the proper intensity of effort, scanty results will be produced by any amount of exercise, and certainly none in the areas of muscular size and strength. Given the proper intensity, however, a small amount of exercise will give the best possible results.

Although this has been pointed out repeatedly to bodybuilders, it remains largely misunderstood. The usual practice is to do more individual exercises and more sets of each exercise in the mistaken belief that this increase in amount of exercise will also produce an increase in intensity of effort.

HARDER IS BETTER

As bodybuilders know too well, it is difficult to perform multiple sets of exercise while exerting maximum intensity in each set. Such a workout quickly degenerates into a form of manual labor. Eventually, such workouts do produce results. The gains, however, result directly from only one or two sets in each workout, regardless of the number of sets actually performed. The other sets not only represent wasted effort, but each set performed beyond the minimum number required actually retards progress.

According to Arthur Jones, "Best results will always be produced by the minimum amount of exercise that imposes the maximum amount of growth stimulation." Any extra exercise that is added to a bodybuilding routine will retard progress, in many cases, by as much as 90%. If carried to extremes, additional exercise will result in losses in both muscular size and strength.

RESEARCH FINDINGS

What is the minimum amount of exercise that will impose the maximum amount of growth stimulation? This problem may never be solved to the satisfaction of everybody. But research provides a few practical guidelines.

Twenty years ago, isometrics were in vogue. All that was required, according to the isometric contraction theory of strength development, was the application of a high percentage of one's existing strength against an unmoving resistance. Isometrics were popular for only a few years because trainees realized that they produced little in the way of results. Yet the theory behind isometrics is basically sound. Unfortunately, the conclusions that were drawn from the research that provided the basis of that theory ignored several other well-established facts. A cold muscle is incapable of working within its existing level of reserve strength. Unless a work load is heavy enough to force the muscles to work well inside their reserve levels of strength, few results will be produced. Before a muscle is capable of a maximum effort, it must be warmed up through the performance of several repetitions of a movement that is lighter than it is capable of handling. If not warmed up, the muscle will fail at a level far below its actual strength. So an isometric effort, even if carried to the point of muscular failure, does not provide much in the way of growth stimulation; the effort is simply not great enough to force the muscles to work inside their existing levels of strength reserve. Thus, a bodybuilder using isometrics or static contractions can work repeatedly to the point of muscular failure and produce little in the way of results.

This does not mean that the isometric theory is worthless. On the contrary, some aspects of it are worthy of being included in any bodybuilding program. Isometric contractions should be made against an unmoving resistance in every set of almost every exercise, but only after the maximum number of full movements have been performed. After 12 or more repetitions, the muscles involved are so exhausted that they are momentarily incapable of moving the resistance—in spite of a 100% effort.

Then and only then should isometric contractions be done. Without this final effort, it is impossible to induce maximum growth stimulation.

PUTTING FACTS INTO PRACTICE

In practice, a set of 10 repetitions in the curl is performed as follows: The first four repetitions are performed very

Do *not* terminate an exercise simply because the movements become very hard or because the muscle starts to ache. An exercise is *properly* terminated only when the involved muscles are momentarily exhausted to the point at which another repetition is impossible in spite of maximum effort. (Photo by Inge Cook)

slowly as a warm-up. The next four repetitions are done slightly faster, but still smoothly and slowly. The ninth repetition would be slower and the tenth would be the slowest of all, the muscles involved being almost completely fatigued. The eleventh repetition would not be successful. Somewhere along the range of movement in the eleventh repetition, the muscles will fail completely and no additional upward movement will be possible. At this position the muscles will be contracting as hard as possible against a heavy resistance, but no movement will occur. After this brief isometric contraction the exercise is terminated.

To repeat, it is impossible for a bodybuilder to build muscular size or strength by performing that which he is already capable of doing easily. He must attempt the momentarily impossible, and such attempts should involve maximum efforts. But those efforts should be performed only after the muscles have been warmed up and only after they have been worked to the point of momentary exhaustion.

10

building strength, not demonstrating it

A workout is one thing; a competitive weightlifting meet is a different matter. The best way to *build* strength has little in common with the best way to *demonstrate* strength. Yet many bodybuilders make the mistake of training as if they were in a weightlifting contest, perhaps being more interested in impressing their associates than in trying to build muscular size and strength.

Olympic lifters and power lifters must practice maximum, single-attempt lifts, both in training and in competition. But there is no reason for bodybuilders ever to attempt heavy singles. While maximum muscular size cannot be produced without maximum muscular strength, it does not follow that building strength requires heavy single-attempt lifts. On the contrary, greater strength and size will result from the performance of repetitions within the 8 to 12 range.

An Olympic weightlifter is shown successfully jerking 456.5 pounds. Weightlifters must practice maximum single-attempt lifts. Bodybuilders should avoid such movements. (Photo by Ellington Darden)

CONTROLLED REPETITIONS

Maximum size and strength can be produced without ever exerting maximum force, even though maximum contraction force is a requirement for maximum growth stimulation. For growth stimulation, it is only necessary to produce momentary maximum contraction force. This can and should be done only after your momentary ability has been reduced by the performance of at least three repetitions that did not involve maximum contraction force. In effect, by the time you produce maximum force, your momentary ability will be reduced to the point at which the danger of injury is greatly reduced.

In practice, you should use a weight with which you can perform several consecutive repetitions. The first three or four repetitions should be performed at a reduced speed, since contraction force involves three factors—resistance, distance or vertical movement, and speed of movement. If you reduce the speed of movement, you are reducing the contraction force in direct ratio. Thus, you reduce the danger of injury to an even greater degree because it is not the resistance that causes injury, but rather your attempt to move the resistance. The less contraction force you use, the less likely you are to be injured.

More important, while a reduction in contraction force reduces the pull on the connective tissues in direct ratio, such slow movements also reduce the acceleration factor. A movement involving maximum speed will increase the acceleration factor far more than the actual speed is increased. Inertia is the tendency shown by a moving mass to continue moving, but it is also the tendency for a stationary mass to remain stationary. The forces resulting from a sudden attempt to accelerate a stationary mass enormously increase the jerk imposed on whatever is connecting the source of power and the resistance. In this case the connection is the tendons, the ligaments, and even the muscles themselves.

For example, if 4 units of contraction force applied against an immobile resistance impose 4 units of strain on the connective tissues, 8 units of contraction force applied against the same amount of resistance will not impose 8 units of strain. Instead, it will impose 16 units of strain. And 16 units of contraction force applied against the same resistance will impose 256 units of strain. Thus, increasing the force application by a ratio of 4 to 1 will increase the strain by a ratio of 64 to 1. *So it should be obvious that the danger of injury rises at a much faster rate than the increase in force application.*

FIRST REPETITIONS ARE THE MOST DANGEROUS

Bodybuilders do not hurt themselves during a first repetition because they were not warmed up properly. They hurt themselves because they are strongest at that point in the set. And they make the mistake of moving at maximum speed at a time when this results in more pull and much more jerk from the geometrical increase in the acceleration factor. Since single-attempt lifts are always first repetitions, it should be evident that they are the most dangerous type of movements.

Since maximum growth stimulation can be induced by momentary maximum contraction force, most of the potential danger can be avoided by reducing the existing level of ability before producing maximum force. Once again, you can accomplish this by performing three or four repetitions at a reduced speed immediately prior to a maximum movement. Or it can be accomplished by pre-exhausting the muscles by working them in an isolated fashion immediately prior to involving them in a heavier compound movement.

Since the ability of the muscles to increase their strength is apparently disproportionate to the ability of the connective tissues to increase their resistance to strain, injuries will eventually result if you make a practice of producing maximum force during your first repetitions or if you attempt heavy singles. Competitive lifters, therefore, are almost certain to hurt themselves sooner or later, and in their cases,

A maximum attempt in the bench press, or any other exercise, is not only unproductive for building muscle but also dangerous. (Photo by Ellington Darden)

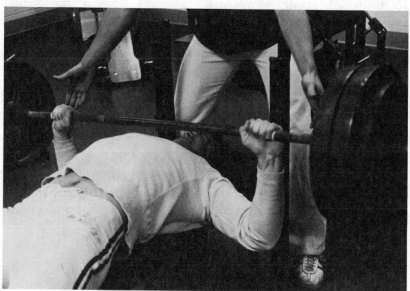

this risk cannot be avoided. Still, they should be aware of the hazard involved.

It does not follow that competitive lifters cannot reduce their risk. They can—and to a great degree—by supporting heavy weights in a variety of positions. This will increase the connective strength of tendons and ligaments.

LAST REPETITIONS ARE THE SAFEST

Most bodybuilders believe that they are avoiding injury if they terminate a set prior to the most difficult repetitions. They consider the last repetitions the most dangerous. In fact, the opposite is true. The farther you progress into a set, the safer the work.

Regardless of the number of repetitions involved in a set, the first repetition is always the most dangerous and the last repetition is always the safest. The more difficult it feels, the safer it is. The more dangerous it seems, the safer it is.

The last of 10 repetitions, for example, feels harder to do because you are almost exhausted by the time you reach that point in the set. You do not feel your actual output; instead you feel the percentage of your momentarily possible output. If you can press 200 pounds, then 100 pounds will feel light to you during a first repetition and will feel heavier during each following repetition. By the time you reach a point at which you are capable of performing one more repetition, the 100 pounds will feel very heavy. At that moment the 100 pounds you are lifting will actually be very heavy, since it will momentarily require 100% of your strength to move it.

Everything is relative insofar as feelings are concerned. The danger of injury, however, is not related directly to those feelings. Instead, your connective tissues have an actual level of resistance to pull, and since they do not perform work in the sense that they do not contract like muscles, their resistance is not reduced during the performance of a set of several repetitions. If a particular tendon has an existing level of resistance capable of withstanding 100 units of pull, then that level of resistance remains constant throughout a set. It will be 100 units during the first repetition and 100 units during the tenth repetition. Yet, the danger factor changes. During a first repetition you might be momentarily capable of exerting 200 units of pull. If you do so, then an injury will surely result. By the time you reach the tenth repetition, however, your momentary ability may be reduced to only 10 units of pull. At that point you are not strong enough to hurt yourself.

Unfortunately, most bodybuilders avoid the most productive repetitions in all their sets because of an unjustified fear of injury. After working right up to the point at which one or two more repetitions would have done them some good, they stop. They are actually avoiding the safest repetitions of all, the only ones capable of producing the stimulation of muscle growth that they seek.

11

proper form

The style of performance is very important if maximum benefit is to be obtained from a bodybuilding program. Proper form includes isolation of the involved muscles, relaxation of the uninvolved muscles, speed of movement, range of movement, and supervision.

ISOLATION OF THE INVOLVED MUSCLES

An isolation movement is an exercise that involves only one muscle group or one part of the body. Under ideal conditions an isolation movement provides rotation around only one joint. It involves a single-joint rotary movement. Only a few barbell exercises, such as the wrist curl and calf raise, provide effective rotary movement. Most of the Nautilus machines, however, do supply rotary movement, which is necessary for muscle isolation.

A compound movement works several muscle groups or

In performing a single-joint movement for the biceps, such as the standing barbell curl, it is important not to cheat or bring into action other muscles. Stand as tall as possible and curl the barbell smoothly and slowly.

parts of the body. Movement occurs around two or more joints. The bench press, squat, and deadlift are examples of compound exercises.

The preferred choice with barbells, because of their limitations, are compound movements. With Nautilus equipment, however, the bodybuilder can perform both single-joint rotary movements and multiple-joint compound movements.

Regardless of the exercise or the equipment, you should concentrate on isolating only the muscles involved in a specific movement. You should always do as many repetitions in perfect form as possible. Cheating, or bringing into action surrounding muscle groups, should be kept to a minimum. The only time cheating is permissible is on compound exercises, when no other perfect repetitions can be performed. Two or three additional repetitions can be cheated. But, even then, the bodybuilder should cheat the absolute minimum amount required.

RELAXATION OF UNINVOLVED MUSCLES

Most bodybuilders are aware of the importance of choosing exercises that isolate specific muscle groups as much as possible. What many may not be aware of, however, is that isolation of a particular muscle is directly related to the ability to relax the uninvolved muscles.

If you perform leg extensions for the quadriceps muscles, it is to your advantage to relax the upper body. Excessive gripping with the hands involves many muscles of the forearms and upper arms. Moving the torso forward or sideways brings into action the abdominals or obliques. Even tensing the jaws, squinting the eyes, groaning, or yelling during an exercise can weaken the neurological input to a given area of the body. The bodybuilder's intention in performing leg extensions is to build muscular size and strength in the quadriceps. Relaxing all other muscles while slowly contracting the quadriceps will help involve the maximum number of fibers.

Intense stress placed on too many muscles at the same time is both unproductive and dangerous. Headaches during exercise are often a first sign of your inability to relax uninvolved muscles. You can release greater energy to the isolated muscle by learning to relax your other body parts. This allows for more efficient growth stimulation.

SPEED OF MOVEMENT

A force plate is a delicate measuring device that can be connected to an oscilloscope. Accurate measurements of force during a barbell exercise can be recorded by standing on the plate as you perform an exercise. The difference between the performance of fast and slow repetitions, as recorded on the screen, is dramatic.

Fast repetitions produce peaks and drops on the oscilloscope. These peaks and drops indicate that a 100-pound barbell, while being lifted, can exert from more than 500 pounds of force to less than zero. Such erratic force is not only unproductive as far as muscle stimulation is concerned but is also very dangerous to the joints, muscles, and connective tissues.

Slow, steady repetitions produce a relatively smooth tracing on the oscilloscope. This kind of tracing indicates that the barbell's resistance is being directed properly against the muscle throughout the exercise's range of movement.

Pictured above is a subject standing on a force plate that is connected to an oscilloscope. The forces are recorded as the subject performs an overhead press. If the pressing movement is performed in a smooth, steady manner, the bleep in the middle of the screen will travel across the oscilloscope in a relatively straight line. If the barbell is pressed in a fast, jerky style, the bleep will move wildly up and down the oscilloscope, thereby accurately indicating the changing levels of force imposed on the subject. Below: an actual tracing of the changing forces involved in rapid exercise. Notice the peaks and valleys in the tracing. A sixty-pound barbell, when suddenly jerked or thrown, can exert a force of several hundred pounds or a force that literally measures below zero. Such rapid exercise is not only unproductive as far as muscle building is concerned, but it is also very dangerous to the joints, muscles, and connective tissues. (Photos by Inge Cook)

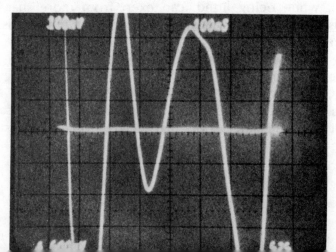

The research performed at Nautilus Sports/Medical Industries over the last 10 years proves that slow repetitions are much more productive than fast repetitions for bodybuilding purposes. As a general rule, each repetition should be performed in approximately six seconds: two seconds to lift the weight, four seconds to lower it. The negative or lowering phase of each repetition should be emphasized.

RANGE OF MOVEMENT

The range of movement of each repetition, from full extension to full flexion, should be as great as possible. When it contracts even a little, a muscle must produce movement. If it contracts fully, that muscle must produce a full range of movement. If the movement resulting from muscular contraction is less than full range, the entire length of the muscle will not be involved in the work. Increased muscular size and shape are most likely to be achieved when the muscles have been strengthened in every position over a full range of movement.

SUPERVISION

A bodybuilder is rarely able to push himself to a 100% effort. He may succeed in two or three exercises, but experience teaches that it is virtually impossible to do this consistently. High-intensity exercise is not easy. Properly performed, it is very demanding, and it is not surprising that few people can do it on their own. A supervisor or training partner is usually needed to urge bodybulders to work at the required level of intensity.

An example from the sport of running should help clarify this concept. Let us say that an athlete can run a quarter mile in 50 seconds. When he runs at this speed he is making a 100% effort. His pain during the last 100 yards will be almost unbearable. He rationalizes, therefore, that if he slows slightly to run the distance in 55 seconds, he will probably get about 90% results. If he repeats this 55-second quarter three times, he reasons, he will be accomplishing more than he would by running once around the track in an all-out 100% effort. And it will certainly hurt less.

Actually, his reasoning is false. His three runs at 55 seconds per quarter will never produce as good results as a single all-out run that uses 100% of his effort. It is the 100% effort that forces his body to overcompensate and become stronger. Ninety-percent efforts, regardless of how many times they are repeated, will never produce the results attained by one 100% effort.

The same principle applies to building strength. If a bodybuilder can do 11 repetitions in a strenuous effort on a given exercise, but stops at 10, he has not reached his potential. This is why supervision is so important. You simply cannot push yourself hard enough. You need a supervisor to tell you when to slow down, to hold your head back, and to relax your lower body when working your upper body. You must constantly be reminded to eliminate excessive gripping and facial grimaces. You must be urged, implored, and inspired to do the *last* repetition of each exercise.

Regardless of age or strength level, most trainees need supervision during every workout. Without supervision, most bodybuilders will invariably make their exercises easier rather than harder. (Photo by Inge Cook)

12

duration and frequency of workouts

A common, though erroneous theory among bodybuilders states that if some exercise is good, more is better. During World War II, many large-scale exercise experiments were conducted. They all pointed to one major conclusion: There is a definite limit on the amount of exercise that will produce beneficial results. Carried beyond that point, exercise will reverse its benefits, turning them into losses in weight, condition, and stamina.

WIDESPREAD CONFUSION

Since then, other research has shown that it is almost impossible to overwork the body insofar as intensity of effort is concerned. To many people, these conclusions seem to be contradictory. In fact, this is not the case; the problem is one of nomenclature and definition. The phrase *amount of exercise* has been confused with *intensity of effort*.

That confusion has spread, reaching enormous proportions. Today, thousands of bodybuilders are training as many as 20 or more hours weekly, sometimes for years, in attempts to improve their progress. Modern research reveals that far better results would be produced if their training were limited to a maximum of not more than two hours of weekly exercise. But, because even marathon bodybuilding programs will produce good results if continued long enough, it is almost impossible to convince people who have trained that way that even better results would have been produced by briefer workouts. Therefore, most bodybuilders become addicted to long, multiple-set routines, and their results are secondary at best.

FOUR HOURS A DAY

A recent article in a muscle magazine described the training program that a certain bodybuilder followed for a period of seven years, four hours a day, seven days a week— 28 hours of weekly training. His results were fairly good. But Arthur Jones of Nautilus knows that better results would have come sooner from a training routine requiring about 10% of the time that this individual devoted to his training.

Bodybuilding requirements vary with the individual, but they do not vary as much as 1,000%. The bodybuilder in question succeeded merely because he developed a tolerance for this amount of exercise.

NAUTILUS RESEARCH

What does Nautilus research say about duration and frequency? In the 1940s and 1950s, Arthur Jones experimented on himself by trying various weight training systems. Though he discovered many worthwhile benefits, he also got the feeling that something was wrong. Initially, Jones had settled on a training routine that seldom varied. He trained three times weekly for a period of more than three hours during each workout. He did 12 basic barbell exercises and performed four sets of each exercise, for a total of 48 sets. The number of repetitions in each set normally ranged from 8 to 10. He always trained as hard as possible and discontinued an exercise only when he reached a point of momentary muscular failure.

"Even a few weeks of such training would rapidly increase my body weight to a level of 172 pounds," Jones recalls. "But no amount of training would produce the slightest evidence of progress beyond that point."

Jones trained in this fashion sporadically for more than 15 years. Each time, he would reach a plateau at 172 pounds. In frustration he finally decided to try something new. He cut his workouts in half; he reduced his training time by exactly 50%. Instead of performing four sets of each exercise, he performed only two sets.

Within a week Jones found he had added nearly 10 pounds to his body weight and reached a muscular size and strength level that he had previously been unable to attain.

Thinking about the implications of these developments, Jones decided to use only two sets of eight exercises. "The change in the production of results was almost more than I could believe," he notes. "While training only a third as much, I produced far better results. Growth was apparent as a result of every single workout."

Jones concluded that his longer workouts had been *stimulating* growth, but that they had not been *permitting* growth, at least not beyond a certain point. In short, he had created the need for growth, but he had somehow denied his muscles the means to attain it.

Looking back on Jones's initial accomplishments in the field of exercise, one prominent observer has called him "the Thomas Edison of muscle building." He has an inquisitive mind. He is a self-made millionaire. But he is, above all, a thinker.

As Jones experimented on his own body, studying the sources of muscular strength, he came to several logical conclusions concerning physical law and recovery ability.

PHYSICAL LAW

From his own experience, and from the experiences of many other people, Jones knew that a very rapid rate of muscular growth was possible. Why, then, couldn't such a rate of growth be maintained right up to the point of an individual's potential?

A physical law simply states that a given set of circumstances will invariably produce a particular result. If the law is valid, then the result *must* be produced. If the expected result is not forthcoming, then the only logical conclusion is that the circumstances were not those that were required.

If an individual does something once, and a particular result is produced, then the same result should always be produced. If it is not, then that is proof that the circumstances were changed, even though such a change may have escaped attention.

In Jones's case, a certain type and amount of exercise had produced a particular result—for a while and up to a point. Beyond that point the same type and amount of exercise had produced no apparent result at all. It had to follow, then, that some factor had been changed.

RECOVERY ABILITY

Eventually Jones realized that the change had occurred within his own body's system. Growth was produced as long as he worked within the limits imposed by his recovery ability. But when the demands exceeded the ability of his system to meet them, growth became impossible.

A certain balance was obviously required. If the body's recovery ability remained in excess of the demands on it, then growth would occur. But if demands exceeded the body's recovery ability, growth was impossible, regardless of the stimulation provided.

Practical experience also made it obvious that increases in strength resulting from exercise were not matched by equal increases in recovery ability. In effect, as an individual became stronger, he worked closer to the limits of his recovery ability. Eventually he would reach a point at which his recovery ability was entirely dissipated by his workout, leaving nothing for growth.

Realizing that a constantly depleted recovery ability made growth impossible, and being unable to increase his recovery ability, Jones's only remaining choice was to reduce the demands his workouts were making on his body. When this reduction was made, the result was immediate growth.

THE COLORADO EXPERIMENT

When Jones developed the basic Nautilus machines in the early 1970s, he found that they worked the muscles much more thoroughly than barbells. This fact led him to the realization that training time could be reduced sharply. "Just how little exercise is actually required?" was the question he asked himself.

Under controlled conditions at Colorado State University in May of 1973, with the supervision of Dr. Elliott Plese, director of the exercise physiology laboratory at Colorado State, Jones trained Casey Viator in a famous project called "The Colorado Experiment."

Over a 28-day period, Viator performed 14 workouts. A typical workout consisted of one set of 12 different Nautilus machine exercises and an average training session lasted only 33.6 minutes.

The results were spectacular. In 28 days Viator gained 63.21 pounds of muscle mass and lost 17.93 pounds of body fat. His body weight increased from 166.87 pounds to 212.15 pounds. His average muscle mass gain for each of his 14 workouts was 4.51 pounds.

Part of Viator's phenomenal gain in muscle mass was due to the fact that he was rebuilding previously existing levels of muscular size. On December 23, 1972, Viator weighed

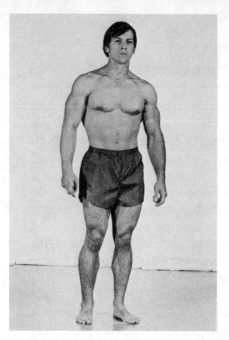
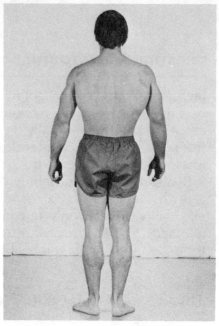

On May 1, 1973, Casey Viator weighed 166.87 pounds. His percentage of body fat, as measured by the "potassium 40 whole body counter" at Colorado State University, was 13.8 percent. (Photos by Inge Cook)

On May 28, 1973, Casey Viator weighed 212.15 pounds with 2.47 percent body fat. As a result of fourteen Nautilus training sessions, Viator increased his body weight by 45.28 pounds and lost 17.93 pounds of body fat. His overall muscle mass gain in twenty-eight days was a phenomenal 63.21 pounds. (Photos by Inge Cook)

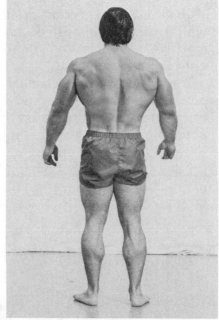

200.5 pounds. In early January of 1973 he was involved in a serious accident at work and lost most of one finger. Several days later he almost died from an allergic reaction to an antitetanus injection. For the next four months he did not train. Since his activity level was low, his food intake was reduced accordingly. During that four-month period he lost 33.63 pounds, 18.75 of the pounds being attributed to the nearly fatal injection. So his loss from nearly four months out of training totaled 14.88 pounds, or less than a pound a week.

Thus, even though Viator was rebuilding part of his muscle mass, the experiment clearly demonstrated that proper training would produce rapid but steady increases in muscular weight.

TWELVE EXERCISES, THREE TIMES A WEEK

As a result of The Colorado Experiment and other related research, Jones decided that the ideal bodybuilding workout

Dr. Elliott Plese, director of the exercise physiology laboratory at Colorado State University, is shown monitoring Casey Viator as he performs negative-only triceps extensions. The trainee performs the positive portion of the exercise with his legs and the negative phase with his arms. (Photo by Inge Cook)

on Nautilus equipment should consist of no more than one set of 12 different exercises, performed progressively at high intensity, lasting less than 30 minutes.

Once any high-intensity workout has been completed, the body needs at least 48 hours to overcompensate and get stronger. Thus, a bodybuilder should *not* train on consecutive days. An every-other-day schedule is enough.

Everything has a price, and everything has a value. If the price paid of many hours, seven days a week, is really required, then the results are simply not worth it. In fact, the actual price that one must pay to develop maximum muscular size and strength is really very low.

Eventually, this will be understood by all bodybuilders. In the meantime, millions of hours of training are being wasted. It is a tragedy that so many bodybuilding coaches and proprietors of gymnasiums are mistakenly doing more to prevent their trainees from achieving success than they are in the direction of producing results.

negative-only exercise

Until 1972, few, if any, bodybuilders had ever tried negative-only exercise. In the fall of that year Arthur Jones wrote an article that startled bodybuilders by challenging them to think not in terms of how much you can lift, but in terms of how much you can *lower.*

By chance, a well-known physiologist read that article and was impressed. Later he attended the 1972 Olympic Games in Munich, West Germany. A Dr. Paavo Komi, professor of physiology at the University of Jyvaskyla, was addressing the Olympic Scientific Congress on the same subject. Dr. Komi reported that he had used the negative-only concept to train some of his Scandinavian weightlifters. He was convinced that negative training would turn them into winners. Several days later one Scandinavian athlete won a gold medal and two won bronzes.

After returning from Europe, the physiologist phoned Arthur Jones about his conversations with Dr. Komi. To his surprise, Jones had carried his negative research much further than anyone else in the world. He had built many special machines and embarked on numerous large-scale studies. He had become a devout believer in this unprecedented method for exercising the muscles.

To understand these concepts, a discussion of various types of strength is necessary.

TYPES OF STRENGTH

There are three types of strength:

1. *Positive strength:* The muscle is shortening against resistance.

2. *Holding strength:* The muscle is exerting force, but very limited movement is occurring.

3. *Negative strength:* The muscle is lengthening against resistance.

Using the barbell in a strength test, let us assume that an average trainee can curl 100 pounds in a maximum effort. Therefore, his *positive* strength in the curl is 100 pounds. If he can curl 100 pounds, then we know from many tests that the average trainee can hold 120 in the midrange position. Thus, his *holding* strength is 120 pounds. If he can curl 100 pounds and hold 120 pounds, our research indicates that he can successfully lower 140 in a smooth and steady fashion. So his *negative* strength is said to be 140 pounds.

The above example reveals that a bodybuilder of average neuromuscular efficiency can *hold* 20% more resistance than he can lift. He can *lower* 20% more than he can hold or 40% more than he can lift. Clearly, a bodybuilder's negative strength is much greater than his positive strength.

If skill is removed from a strength test, Nautilus research has discovered that increasing either positive or negative strength always results in a corresponding increase in the other. Our research over the last eight years has also shown that concentrating on the negative phase of a movement produces better results than emphasizing the positive phase. This is a discovery of the utmost importance to the sport of bodybuilding.

NEGATIVE-ONLY RESEARCH

In 1972 and 1973, Nautilus conducted many lengthy tests that involved purely negative work or negative-only exercise. The positive part of the exercise was removed entirely. This was not done because positive work was bad, but because it was necessary to eliminate the positive work in order to be sure that the research produced results that were in fact a product of negative work only.

It should be pointed out here that negative-only training, as it applies to some exercises, is not practical. In these cases it is not practical because it requires several helpers who are needed to lift the weight so that the trainee can perform only the negative or lowering phase of the exercise.

The test subjects were bodybuilders, football players, other athletes, and a few nonathletes. In every single case the results were astonishing. Muscle growth was rapid in all subjects. Strength increases exceeded expectations.

NEGATIVE-ONLY GUIDELINES

In the testing program only three workouts were conducted each week. Most trainees used 10 exercises during each session, with some subjects performing only 8 or 9. A few subjects performed as many as 12.

From 8 to 12 repetitions were done during each set. When it was possible for a subject to perform as many as 12 repetitions in good form, resistance was increased.

Only one set of each exercise was performed. An entire workout might consist of as few as 64 repetitions (8 repetitions of each of 8 exercises). Or a maximum length workout might include up to 144 repetitions (12 repetitions of each of 12 exercises).

Performed in that format, an exercise set required approximately two minutes with little rest permitted between exercises. Thus, an entire workout usually required 18 to 20 minutes, but never more than 30 minutes.

Barbells and Nautilus machines were both used. The exercises performed were as follows:

A negative-only bench press is being performed with 500 pounds. A bodybuilder will be able to lower approximately 40 percent more weight than he can lift. (Photo by Art Johnson)

Conventional Equipment	Nautilus Machines
Bench press	Hip and Back
Press behind neck, seated	Leg Extension
Shoulder shrug	Leg Curl
Chin	Pullover
Dip	Behind-Neck
Stiff-legged deadlift	Torso-Arm
	Rowing Torso
	Biceps Curl
	Triceps Extension

Speed was purposely slow. The subjects permitted the weight to move slowly to the bottom position, resisting the pull of gravity and not permitting the weight to drop. A normal repetition required 10 to 15 seconds for the lowering movement. During the first 2 or 3 repetitions it would have been possible for our subjects to have stopped the downward movement. But no attempt to stop was made. Instead, the weight was permitted to move slowly.

After a few repetitions if the weight had been selected correctly, it became impossible to stop the downward movement. From that point until the end of the exercise the trainee tried as hard as possible to stop the movement. An exercise was finished only when he was trying with all his

Negative-only barbell training requires the use of several assistants who must raise the barbell in perfect rhythm. T-bars built out of pipes to fit over the ends of the barbell will greatly facilitate the assistants' control of a heavy weight. (Photo by Art Johnson)

strength but was failing. In other words, the entire lowering movement was completed in two or three seconds, in spite of a subject's best efforts to stop it.

To summarize, a properly performed set of a negative-only exercise consisted of a few initial repetitions, during which the trainee could have stopped the movement but did not try, followed by other repetitions during which he tried as hard as possible to stop the movement but failed.

Altogether, the test subjects performed several man years of this training over a period of six months; the results were always outstanding. A few examples will prove the point.

Negative-only leg curls can be performed by having two assistants do the positive or lifting part of each repetition for the trainee. The trainee then lowers the weight very slowly to the stretched position.

One member of a Canadian professional football team became so strong in the negative pullover exercise that he was using 675 pounds for several repetitions. Two months earlier he could handle only 275 pounds on the same exercise.

A defensive lineman from the Buffalo Bills trained negatively for two months and added 20 pounds of muscle to his 6-foot, 7-inch frame. In addition, he cut a full two-tenths from his already fast time in the 40-yard dash, added 5½ inches to his vertical jump, and doubled his strength in five major muscle groups: hips, thighs, chest, upper back, and neck.

A strong, young bodybuilder initially performed 32 repetitions in the leg press with 400 pounds. After training negatively for four weeks, he performed 45 repetitions with 840 pounds on the leg press under the same testing conditions. And he was forced to quit because of pain rather than muscular failure.

TWO SECONDS UP, FOUR SECONDS DOWN

Probably the most important thing learned was the fact that athletes have been neglecting the negative aspect of exercise for years and that their results have suffered as a consequence. In particular, bodybuilders should pay careful attention to *both* the positive and negative parts of all exercises.

Even in normal positive-negative sets, the weight should be lifted smoothly and *slowly*. Then it should be lowered to the starting position even *more slowly*. An excellent guideline to follow is that it should take two seconds to lift the resistance and four seconds to lower it—two seconds positive, four seconds negative. Doing exercises in this fashion will require you to use less weight, but it will greatly increase the results, which is what you are after. As a side benefit, this training style will almost totally eliminate the chance of injury.

14

negative-accentuated exercise

Many bodybuilders make the mistake of paying too much attention to the positive part of their exercises but then ignore the negative part. They lift the weight in good form, but they lower it in a haphazard manner.

For the purpose of increasing muscular size and strength, the negative phase is the most important. To the degree that it is possible, the negative part of the exercise should be emphasized.

ADVANTAGES OF NEGATIVE WORK

The negative phase of exercise provides the following advantages: (1) stretching, for the improvement of flexibility; (2) prestretching, for high-intensity muscular contraction; (3) resistance in the position of full contraction, for full-range exercise, and (4) maximum application of resistance throughout a full range of possible movement, which results from the fact that it is impossible to throw a weight down.

The first three advantages of negative training are easy to understand. Without the back pressure of force pulling against you at the begining of an exercise movement, there would be nothing to stretch your muscles and improve flexibility. Without such stretching of the muscles, there would be no prestretch, which is the neurological stimulus required for high-intensity muscular contraction. With no force pulling back against you at the end of an exercise movement, there is no resistance in the position of full muscular contraction. Thus, without negative work, nothing would be done for flexibility. High-intensity work would be impossible, as would full-range exercise.

The fourth advantage requires more explanation. While performing positive work it is easy to throw the weight rather than lift it. If the upward movement is started with a jerk, or if the movement is done too quickly, your muscles will not be able to keep pace with the weight. Having started with a yank, which is dangerous in itself, the muscles you seek to exercise can contribute only a little to the subsequent movement. When this happens your muscles are deprived of a most valuable phase of the exercise.

A weight that is too heavy may make it impossible for you to lift it properly. So, instead of lifting it, you are forced to throw it. This results in an unproductive and dangerous style of training.

The weight should be as heavy as possible but not too heavy. It should be as heavy as you can handle in good form. If it is heavier than that, good form becomes impossible and injury probable. If the weight is lighter than that, you are simply wasting time and futilely burning up energy. You should use as much weight as you can, while maintaining good form. You should increase the weight as often and as much as you can. But you should never increase the weight if you must sacrifice form to do so.

In the real world, eager bodybuilders often start throwing the weight instead of lifting it. Usually, they are under the impression that they are showing progress, since it soon becomes possible to use more weight.

By using a negative style of training, such throwing becomes unlikely. You can always drop a weight, but you cannot throw it down.

SLOW, CONTROLLED REPETITIONS

In negative-only training, the weight must be lifted by somebody else; then you slowly lower the weight, performing only the negative part of the work. Jerking, yanking, heaving, throwing, and too-fast movements are thus avoided. The objective of negative exercise is to lower the weight slowly, very slowly, but without interrupting the downward movement. To repeat, at the start of a negative-only exercise you should be able to stop the downward movement if you try to, but you should not try. After six or seven repetitions you should be unable to stop the downward movement no matter how hard you try; however, you should still be able to guide it into a slow, steady, smooth descent.

Finally, after two or three more repetitions you should find it impossible to stop the weight's downward acceleration. At that moment, you should terminate the exercise.

Properly performed negative-only exercise, therefore, assures full-range exercise for the muscles because the weight is never thrown. It always moves at a smooth, steady pace.

THE PROBLEM OF HELPERS

Negative-only exercise is not without problems. One problem results from the fact that it is usually necessary to have somebody lift the weight for you so that you can perform only the lowering part.

A few exercises can be performed in a negative-only fashion without help. Negative chins can be done by climbing into the top position using the legs, so that the arms simply lower you back down. Negative dips can be done in the same way.

In performing a negative-only chin, the legs are used to perform the positive part of the exercise, and the arms and torso are employed in the negative phase. (Photo by Ellington Darden)

Depending on the availability of certain Nautilus machines, a few other exercises can be done in a negative-only fashion without help. In general, however, you will need help—and finding such help is seldom easy. For most bodybuilders a totally negative program of exercises is impractical. That is why negative-accentuated training was invented.

NEGATIVE-ACCENTUATED TRAINING

Negative-accentuated training does not require helpers. Nor does it require nearly as much resistance as negative-only training. All you need is some Nautilus or other machines that have single-connected movement arms.

The leg extension machine offers a good example of negative-accentuated exercise. If you can normally handle 100 pounds for 10 repetitions, you should use 70 pounds. In

To perform negative-accentuated work on a Nautilus machine, the trainee should use approximately 70 percent of the resistance that he normally handles for eight to twelve repetitions. He lifts the resistance with two limbs and lowers it very slowly with only one limb. (Photo by Ellington Darden)

other words, use 70% of the weight you would normally use.

Lift the movement arm with both legs. Pause in the contracted position and smoothly transfer the resistance from both legs to the right leg. Slowly lower the right leg over about 8 seconds. Lift the weight back to the top position with both legs, pause, and lower again, this time with the left leg, in a slow, even manner. Up with two, down with one; up with two again, down with the other. You should continue until you can no longer raise the weight to the contracted position.

If the weight is selected correctly, you should reach a point of momentary failure at about the eleventh or twelfth lifting repetition. When you can perform 12 repetitions, you should increase the resistance by 5%. A properly performed set of negative-accentuated exercise will consist of 8 to 12 lifting movements, plus 4 to 6 negative movements performed by the right leg and an equal number by the left.

Two other popular Nautilus machines that may be used in a negative-accentuated manner are the double shoulder (overhead press) and multi-biceps. (Photos by Ellington Darden)

Other negative-accentuated exercises that can be performed on various machines are the leg curl, leg press, calf raise, pullover, overhead press, decline press, biceps curl, and triceps extension.

In exercising, form or style may not seem important, but it is certainly a prerequisite for optimum results. Using good form with too little weight can accomplish little of value. And using too much weight without good form is even worse. But if you select the correct weight and use it in a negative-accentuated program, you will be rewarded with not only good form but with outstanding results as well.

15

indirect effect

Throw a stone into a pool of water and it will make a splash. Also, a wave will run to the far end of the pool. The larger the stone, the larger the splash and the larger the wave. A similar effect results from exercise. Arthur Jones calls this factor the *indirect effect*.

"When one muscle grows in response to exercise," writes Jones, "the entire muscular structure of the body grows to a lesser degree, even muscles that are not being exercised at all. And the larger the muscle that is growing, or the greater the degree of growth, the greater this indirect effect will be."

In weight training circles this effect is most noticeable as a result of performing full squats with a barbell. Performing squats as a single exercise will induce large-scale muscular growth throughout the body. For example, if a six-foot man weighing 150 pounds is put on a regular schedule of heavy squats, he may gain 30 pounds of muscle mass within a year.

All of this growth, however, will not take place in the legs and the lower back. Considerable growth will also occur in the shoulders, chest, neck, and arms. This individual may have 13-inch upper arms at the beginning of his program, and by the end of his program his arms will probably be at least 15 inches in circumference. Other muscular masses exhibit similar growth to a greater or lesser degree. This happens despite the fact that no direct exercise was performed for them.

While it is possible to build the various muscles disproportionately through the use of an unbalanced exercise program, the body seems to impose a definite limit on this imbalanced development. For example, it is almost impossible to build the size of the arms beyond a certain point unless the large muscles of the legs are also exercised.

A COMMON MISTAKE

Young bodybuilders tend to ignore the development of their legs, concentrating instead on their arms and torso. Such a lopsided program will permit the arms to grow up to a point. Additional growth will not take place, however, until heavy exercises for the legs are added. Then the arms immediately start growing.

While the amount of growth resulting from this factor is not known, it is apparent that it varies within a certain range. Such variation seems to depend on two conditions: (1) The larger the muscle mass exercised, the larger the indirect effect will be. (2) The greater the distance between the muscle that is being exercised and the muscle that is not being exercised, the smaller the indirect effect will be.

Thus, it is clear that working only the arms would have the largest indirect effect on nearby muscular masses such as the deltoids, pectorals, latissimus, and trapezius. And this work would have the least effect on the gastrocnemius muscles of the lower legs. It is also clear that the indirect effect produced by building the arms would not be as great as that resulting from exercising the much larger muscles of the thighs or upper back.

SEQUENCE OF EXERCISE

From the above observations, several important conclusions can be drawn:

1. For maximum bodybuilding, the training program must be well rounded and must include exercises for each of the major muscle masses.

2. The greatest concentration should be directed toward working the largest muscles in the body.

3. The exercise sequence should be arranged so the muscles are worked in the order of their relative sizes, from largest to smallest.

In practice, this last point prescribes that the lower body be worked before the upper body. As a rule, your thighs are exercised before the calves, the back before the chest, and the upper arms before the forearms.

Since the waist muscles are used to stabilize the upper body in most exercises, they should be worked after the arms and forearms. The muscles of the neck, because of their critical location, should be exercised last.

ADVANTAGES OF OVERALL BODY TRAINING

Many authorities have noted that high-intensity work for the major muscle masses results in large-scale growth for those muscles as well as a lower order of growth in other muscles. But nobody knows why. Arthur Jones believes that the indirect effect occurs as a result of a chemical reaction. As a muscle works intensively, a chemical reaction is produced, which spills over and affects the entire body.

Since there is a limit to your overall recovery ability, and since many of the body's chemical functions affect the entire

Greater overall body stimulation will occur if the hips and thighs are trained at the beginning of a workout.

body, it should be evident that training every day is a mistake. Even if a split routine—a training program that works the lower body one day and the upper body the next day—is used, the system cannot recover from a hard workout in fewer than 48 hours. If a high-intensity lower body workout is done between each hard workout for the upper body, the overall system will never be given enough time for full recovery and growth. Even though the trainee who uses a split routine believes he is only working the upper or lower body, this is impossible because of the indirect effect.

Rather than use the indirect effect to your disadvantage, use it to your advantage. Instead of training every day on a split routine, train your body in an overall fashion only three times a week. One set of no more than 12 different exercises, performed every other day, provides the optimum amount of indirect effect.

"Split routines make about as much sense," says Arthur Jones, "as trying to sleep or eat for only one-half of your body. The body should be exercised as a whole."

It cannot be emphasized too often that for bodybuilding purposes, not more than three weekly workouts should be performed—three overall body workouts.

pre-exhaustion principle

The purpose of the pre-exhaustion principle as advocated by Arthur Jones is to overcome one of the defects of almost all barbell exercises. This principle makes it possible to work almost any muscular structure much harder than would normally be possible. In barbell exercises involving two or more muscle groups, a point of failure is reached when the weakest group is no longer able to perform. In this case very little growth stimulation is provided for the stronger muscles involved in the same exercise.

HANDLING THE WEAK LINK

In the barbell squat, for example, a point of failure is usually reached when the lower back muscles fail. This normally happens before the larger and stronger frontal thigh muscles have been worked as hard as is necessary to produce the best possible results. But by pre-exhausting the frontal thigh muscles the problem can be solved. This can be done with standard equipment.

First, perform one set of about 12 repetitions of leg presses, continuing until it is impossible to move the weight in any position. Second, instantly follow the leg presses with a set of about 12 leg extensions, again continuing the set until additional movement is impossible. Third, do barbell squats, but allow no rest following the leg extensions, not even for a second or two.

You will find that very little weight is required for the squats, probably less than half of the amount of weight that is usually used. In many cases, as little as 135 pounds will be required for a man who regularly squats with more than 300 pounds for 12 repetitions.

Regardless of the light weight being used, when you do reach a point of failure in your squats, it will not be because your lower back failed before your thighs were worked properly. When you fail, it will be because your thighs are exhausted. And your thighs will be worked far harder than ever before.

By pre-exhausting your frontal thigh muscles before squatting, you have removed the weak link represented by lower-back involvement in squats.

Another example of the pre-exhaustion principle requires you to perform dumbbell lateral raises immediately before doing behind neck presses. First you perform a set of about 10 repetitions of strict lateral raises with dumbbells, keeping the palms of the hands turned toward the floor rather than permitting them to rotate forward. Maintain a solid lock in your elbows and do not permit your arms to bend. Keeping the arms back in line with the shoulders, you perform the repetitions smoothly and without body swing. You continue with partial repetitions until you cannot lift the dumbbells away from your thighs.

Then, instantly, you do a set of about 10 repetitions of behind neck presses with a grip slightly wider than your shoulders. Again, you carry this exercise to the point of failure.

To pre-exhaust the shoulders with conventional equipment, perform strict dumbbell lateral raises. Then immediately do behind neck presses with a barbell.

So, just as you removed the weak link of your low back muscles through pre-exhaustion in the first example, in the second example you remove your triceps as the weak link in performing an overhead pressing exercise.

Another example is provided by barbell pullovers immediately followed by pulldowns. In this instance you do a set of stiff-armed pullovers and carry them to the point of failure. Then you immediately perform a set of about 12 repetitions of behind neck pulldowns, using a fairly narrow underhanded grip.

Done properly, this cycle will pre-exhaust your latissimus dorsi muscles without tiring your arms. Then, during the brief period in which your arms are actually stronger than your upper back muscles, you can use your arms to work the latissimus muscles much harder than would otherwise be possible.

LESS THAN THREE SECONDS

In all cases the recovery time of pre-exhausted muscles is very brief, usually about three seconds. Thus, you must move instantly from one set of an exercise to the next set of another exercise, with no rest in between, not even as much as two seconds.

This principle can be applied to almost any compound exercise. First, pick the muscle you want to pre-exhaust. Next, pre-exhaust that muscle by performing an isolation-type movement and then instantly involve the same muscle in a compound exercise.

When using this system, you will not be able to use as much weight as you normally would in the follow-up compound exercises, but you will stimulate far more muscle growth.

Other conventional exercises that can be performed in this manner include barbell curls followed by regular-grip chins, triceps extensions followed by parallel dips, stiff-armed supine flies followed by bench presses, bent-forward dumbbell lateral raises followed by barbell rowing motions.

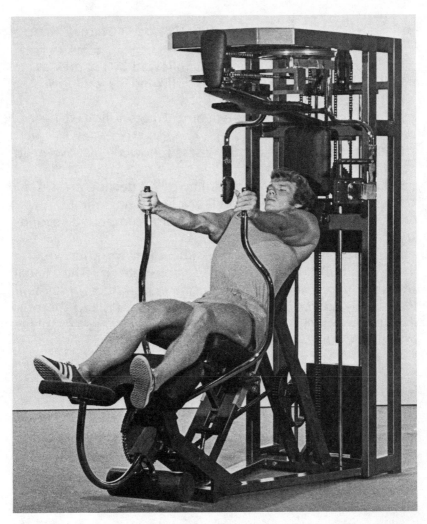

The Nautilus double chest machine makes use of the pre-exhaustion principle. The arm cross isolates the chest muscles without involving the arms. The decline press uses the arms to force the pre-exhausted chest muscles to work even harder. (Photo by Inge Cook)

NAUTILUS DOUBLE MACHINES

The pre-exhaustion principle was used by Arthur Jones when he designed most of his basic Nautilus machines in the early 1970s. Pre-exhaustion techniques may be utilized today on these Nautilus double machines:

Compound Leg—leg extensions followed by leg presses

Pullover/Torso Arm—pullovers followed by pulldowns to the chest

Behind Neck/Torso Arm—behind necks followed by behind neck pulldowns

Double Shoulder—lateral raises followed by overhead presses

Double Chest—arm crosses followed by decline presses

These Nautilus machines all involve a single-joint rotary primary movement plus a multiple-joint compound secondary movement.

Remember that during a pre-exhaustion workout you are trying to build strength, not demonstrate it. The actual amount of weight you move is not important as long as it feels heavy to your muscles. Once you understand the pre-exhaustion principle, you can use it to enormous advantage in almost every workout.

17

genetics and training

Inherited characteristics play a dominant role in every individual's life. These inherited characteristics are transmitted from generation to generation by a complex system of genes.

"How one thinks," Arthur Jones says, "is determined by genetics." Not only is mental capacity determined by genetics, but physical potential such as height, body proportions, fat, muscle mass, and other attributes come to us from our progenitors as well. Obviously, then, great bodybuilders, like musicians, poets, actors, and painters, are born, not made.

Arnold Schwarzenegger, for example, would have never become a physique superstar without well-built ancestors. Lou Ferrigno is certainly not the only six-foot, five-inch man in the world. But his body proportions, neurological efficiency, skeletal formation, lack of body fat, and muscle length combine to make him the largest bodybuilding champion in history. Entirely different genes made Franco

Columbu, at a height of five feet, four inches, one of the greatest bodybuilders in the world.

None of these famous physique champions ever could have attained preeminence in bodybuilding without inherited characteristics. But these inherited traits never would have matured without training. Proper exercise is capable of furnishing correct training for the musculature of any bodybuilder. But training can produce results only within the limits of the individual's inherited capabilities.

BODY PROPORTIONS

Superior athletes have body proportions ideally suited to their particular sport. All-Pro football player Dick Butkus has a long torso, short legs, wide hips, narrow shoulders, and long arms: ideal proportions for a middle linebacker. Olympic champion Jesse Owens had a short torso, narrow hips, long legs, and a favorable ratio of lower to upper leg, all of which gave him the potential to become a very fast sprinter.

Olga Korbut, world champion gymnast, has small proportions that enable her to perform skillfully under limited conditions. Maren Seidler, the women's national shot put champion, has large proportions that fit her sport perfectly. The body proportions essential to Olga would be disastrous to Maren.

From a mechanical point of view, there are body proportions especially suited to bodybuilding. It helps to have broad shoulders, narrow hips, a short torso, medium-length arms, and long legs. Steve Reeves, Mr. America in 1947, had such advantageous proportions, which gave him a distinct edge in physique competition.

Power lifters, on the other hand, are aided by having narrow shoulders, wide hips, a long torso, long arms, and short legs. Vince Anello, world champion in the 198-pound class, is an example of a prototype power lifter. All trainees need to be conscious of such inherited anatomical traits. Appropriate height, torso length, shoulder and hip width,

Vince Anello has ideal body proportions for deadlifting. Notice his short torso and long arms. (Photo by John Balik)

length of arms and legs are crucial determinants of an individual's appearance as well as his ability to perform.

These widths and lengths, the various attachments of tendons to bone, and the strength and musculature of the body are its levers of locomotion. These size relationships are part of the field of physiology called *biomechanics*.

SKELETAL FORMATION

Skeletal formation determines body proportions. A body-builder must possess bones that are large enough to support heavy musculature. But his bones must not exceed a certain size, or he may lose the necessary aesthetic qualities contingent on bone structure. An aspiring bodybuilder with the light bone structure of Johnny Carson could hardly hope to develop the heavy-duty muscles of Lou Ferrigno. Neither can an individual with the gargantuan skeleton of Paul Anderson ever develop the sweeping beauty of Frank Zane. Once a person's bones pass a certain size, the joints tend to become so thick that the taper of a muscle belly cannot fit into them.

The graceful, symmetrical physique of Frank Zane. (Photo by John Balik)

NEUROLOGICAL EFFICIENCY

Neurological efficiency, as it applies to physical strength, is a measurement of the relationship between the nervous system and the muscles. The brain activates those muscles required for any movement, the brain determining the amount of muscle power to apply and selecting it from the available supply of muscular resources. People with high levels of neurological efficiency are able to contract a greater percentage of their muscle masses. This places individuals with lower usable levels at a disadvantage.

Recent research undertaken in Canada reveals that neurological efficiency varies greatly among individuals. In an all-out effort, most people can contract about 30% of a muscle group. A few individuals can manage 40%. Their muscles are no better than others; they merely have the ability to contract a greater percentage of muscle fibers. At the low end of the curve is the 10% person. At the high end is an occasional 50% individual. But for every 50-percenter there is also a 10-percenter. Both of these extremes are rare. A 50-percenter would be a genetic freak in strength. A 10% person would be a motor moron hardly able to walk in a straight line.

These are approximate figures, but an underachieving 50% trainee can often be beaten by a 30% competitor functioning neurologically at his best. The 50% athlete may become so accustomed to coasting that he never learns to make a vigorous effort during training. This is a paradox that often limits performance. With proper understanding, the 50% athlete cannot hide his potential with average performances. Nor can the genetically average athlete defeat the gifted athlete if both have the will to work.

MUSCLE LENGTH

The length of a bodybuilder's muscles is the most important single factor in determining the potential size of those muscles. The longer a person's muscles, the greater the

A 1974 photograph reveals an interesting comparison between the triceps of Richard Baldwin (left) and Mike Mentzer (right). Richard and Mike had the same upper arm measurement, 17¼ inches. Notice, however, that Richard's triceps muscle bellies stop at least two inches short of his elbow, while Mike's continue to the joint. As a result of this additional muscle length, Arthur Jones predicted that Mentzer could have a legitimate 19-inch upper arm (which he now has), but Baldwin would have to be satisfied with a 17¼-inch arm. (Photo by Inge Cook)

cross-sectional area and the volume of his muscles can become.

The most easily measured muscle lengths are the triceps of the arms, the gastrocnemius of the calves, and the flexors of the forearms. When two men flex their triceps, with the arm hanging at their side, and measure the length of the long head of this muscle, vastly different measurements can result. The length of the first man's triceps might measure six inches, while the second man's might be nine inches. The length of the second man's triceps would therefore be 50% greater than the first man's. Consequently, the second man has the potential of 2.25 times as much cross-sectional area (1.5 × 1.5 = 2.25) and 3.375 as much volume or mass (1.5 × 1.5 × 1.5 = 3.375) in his triceps. Untrained, both of these men might have approximately the same arm size, but with proper training the second man can have a much stronger and larger muscle.

If a bodybuilder has a short triceps, it does not mean that all his muscles are short. Differences exist in the same person from one side of the body to the other and from one body part to another. It is a rare individual who has uniform potential over the entire body. Often we see a bodybuilder who has great arms and legs but a weak torso. Then there is the athlete with large thighs and small calves; this is most prevalent among blacks. For reasons unknown, most blacks inherit short gastrocnemius muscles and long tendons in their lower legs. Short gastrocnemius muscles have hindered such superb black bodybuilders as Roy Callendar and Bill Grant from winning major physique championships. Only rarely are long calf muscles found among black bodybuilders, Chris Dickerson and Sergio Oliva being the best-known exceptions.

A study of contrasts between the arms and calves of champion bodybuilders, Bill Grant and Chris Dickerson. Grant (left) inherited long biceps and short gastrocnemius muscles. Dickerson (right) has short biceps and long gastrocnemius muscles. (Photos by John Balik)

The man on the left has medium length biceps and triceps muscles. The man on the right has long biceps and triceps. (Photo by Inge Cook)

Another example of medium muscle bellies (top) and long muscle bellies (bottom), this time in the forearm flexors. Remember, the length of a given muscle determines its potential size. (Photo by Inge Cook)

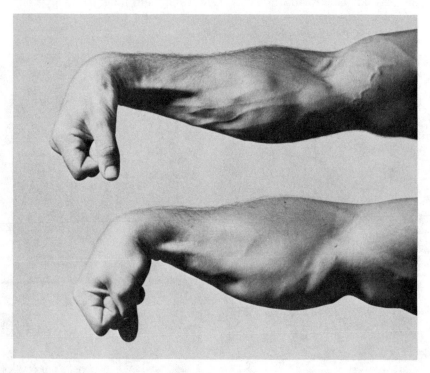

A study of the physique photographs published in body-building magazines over the last 10 years reveals interesting variations between long and short arm muscles. Arnold Schwarzenegger, Bill Pearl, Casey Viator, Mike Mentzer, Boyer Coe, and Sergio Oliva, all have exceedingly long triceps muscles. Larry Scott, Sergio Oliva, Bill Grant, and Lou Ferrigno have biceps muscles that extend almost past the joint. Sergio's biceps, in fact, are so long that he cannot get them into a fully contracted position. Pat Neve has a long biceps and a short triceps. Reg Lewis has just the opposite—a short biceps and a long triceps. Chris Dickerson has medium to short muscles in both his biceps and triceps. Boyer Coe's biceps have an unusual shape: One head of his biceps is long, and the other head is short. This accounts for the high peaked formation of his biceps when they are flexed.

Long muscle bellies in the upper arms, especially the triceps, are an important requirement for exceptional arm measurement. A bodybuilder who desires championship arms must have long muscles, and long muscles are 100% genetic.

BODY FAT

All people are born with adipose cells that specialize in accumulating fat. Many nutrition authorities think that the number of these cells is determined genetically. According to these authorities, family fat depots are inherited in the same way as height, coloring, nose shapes, and muscle lengths.

Researchers have found that the average nonobese person has about 25 to 30 billion fat cells throughout his body. For the moderately obese, the number of fat cells is about 50 billion. For the extremely obese, the number of fat cells may be as high as 237 billion. Perhaps this explains why some people find it very difficult to lose fat permanently.

During the first year of life an infant's cell supply increases rapidly. The total number of fat cells is about three times greater at one year of age than at birth. Scientists believe that most fat cells existing prior to birth are formed during the last three months of pregnancy. After the first year of life the cell number increases more gradually until the age of 10. Fat cells continue to increase until age 13 and again during the growth spurt of adolescence. During adulthood, there is little, if any, increase. In summary, there appear to be three critical periods during which fat cells increase significantly. The first period is the last trimester of pregnancy, the second is the first year of life, and the third occurs during the adolescent growth spurt.

During adulthood the total number of fat cells cannot be altered. It should be said, however, that there is still no substantial data to indicate that the final number of adult fat cells cannot be modified through some form of intervention at an earlier period of life. If fat cell populations can be altered, this probably will be accomplished through a combination of modification of early nutrition and proper exercise.

SKIN COLOR AND MUSCLE DEFINITION

If a computer were programmed to analyze the physical characteristics of the winners of major bodybuilding contests over the last 40 years, an unexpected factor would undoubtedly surface. The vast majority of the winners would have dark eyes, dark hair, and dark skin. A high correlation would exist between low body fat, or muscle definition, and dark skin, eyes, and hair. There would be a few light-skinned, blue eyed, blond-haired bodybuilders, but they would be the exception rather than the rule.

Over many centuries populations have adapted to their geographical locations. Studies have shown that the predominant physical type within any given region will be one that is best suited to the climate. The odds against blond hair being found in a sunny tropical climate are high. Fair-skinned people do not adjust well to hot, open environments unless they spend most of their time indoors. The gene pool in such a climate will contain few genes for blondness but many for dark skin and hair.

Conversely, in cloudy cold countries children with light skin and hair are able to extract more vitamin D from sunlight than can their dark-haired brothers and sisters. Thus, it is the blonds who thrive. Over the centuries, cloudy areas of the world tend to accumulate genes for blondness, whereas genes for dark hair tend to become scarce.

Both heat and cold are stressful to the human body. In fact, a strong relationship seems to exist between body fat and annual mean temperature. The colder the mean temperature, the fatter people become. The warmer the mean temperature, the leaner they are. The relative leanness of warm-dwelling people, and the relative fatness of cold-dwelling people, can be traced back to a period roughly 18,000 to 25,000 years ago. In the cold regions of the world during that time period, the ability to store surplus fat under the skin with the least possible total food intake may have made the difference between life and death.

Central heating, air conditioning, and mass production of warm clothing all serve to minimize a modern individual's exposure to environmental extremes. Even so, scientists can document the extraordinary degree to which the contemporary American still is programmed by blueprints laid down by our Ice Age ancestors.

Among white Americans, obesity is lowest in people of British, Irish, or "old American" origins and is slightly higher in people of Scandinavian and Germanic ancestry. The fattest Americans tend to be people of Balto-Ugric, Central Slav, and Soviet-Russian ancestry.

A striking correlation also exists between body leanness and an individual's city or state. The leanest Americans come from the southeastern United States. The fattest come from the mid-Atlantic states and the Midwest.

What do these findings mean to the bodybuilder? Simply that bodybuilders with dark skin, hair, and eyes—compared to those with light skin, blond hair, and blue eyes—have a genetic advantage where body leanness and extreme muscular definition are concerned.

REALISTIC GOALS

Body proportions, skeletal formation, neurological efficiency, muscle length, body fat, and skin color are all genetic traits that cannot be changed through training. Training can, however, activate them to their maximum capacity. Genetic qualities *are* limiting factors, but this is not to say that a given individual cannot improve his existing development, performance, or appearance. With strict attention paid to training methods and eating habits, and with supervision, every bodybuilder can reach the upper limits of his particular genetic potential.

Even the chosen few who are born with almost perfect combinations of genetic factors required for success will improve faster if they approach their training logically. A would-be champion, whose ultimate potential is less than a rival's, may still achieve greater success through the use of applied intelligence. The ultimate, however, occurs when superior genetic factors are married to the intellectual capacity to utilize them. This combination cannot be beaten.

The following concepts summarize the importance of genetics and bodybuilding:

1. From a biomechanical point of view, there are body proportions and bone structures that are necessary for success in building muscular size and demonstrating strength. There are also ideal body proportions for success in any sport.

2. Individuals with high levels of neurological efficiency obtain faster results from their training. These people also have an advantage in competition, where great muscular strength is required.

3. The length of a given muscle determines its ultimate

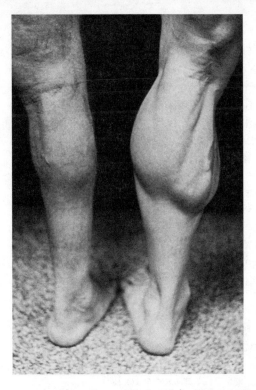

This photograph shows the difference between short and long muscles and their effect on the mass of the calf. The man on the right has greater size to his calf primarily because of his long gastrocnemius and soleus muscles. (Photo by Ellington Darden)

size potential. Bodybuilders desiring large muscle size must be blessed with longer than average muscle bellies.

4. Where an individual stores fat on his body and to what degree are genetically predetermined factors. Many bodybuilders who try to obtain great muscular definition fail to realize that their goal may be impossible. Great muscular definition requires that an individual have a low percentage of body fat and that he store most of his fat around his internal organs. The majority store fat under the skin all over their bodies.

5. Muscle definition, in many respects, is related to skin color. Generally speaking, the darker the skin, the greater the degree of body leanness that can be developed.

BORN, NOT MADE

The superior athlete was born with the genetic possibility of becoming a great basketball player, tennis player, wrestler, runner, bodybuilder, or any kind of sports performer. His training and coaching made his success possible, but they were not as important as genetics.

After watching several professional basketball games, an individual who desired to be taller might assume bouncing a ball would make him taller. After trying various ball-bouncing routines with no success, he might then conclude that bouncing a ball has no effect on his height. He might also realize that if he has the genetic potential to become taller, he will grow tall whether or not he bounces a ball. If he grows in height, it will be because of his genetic inheritance and not his ball bouncing.

To play professional basketball an individual must be very tall. He must learn the skills of basketball at a young age. This is not to say, however, that most people cannot learn the skills of basketball and enjoy playing the game. But there is little chance for an individual to play professional basketball unless he has inherited genes that make him tall.

To win the Mr. America contest or World Bodybuilding Championship an individual must have the *genetic* potential, which is to say that he must have the ideal body proportions and bone structure, long muscle bellies in the appropriate places, and the ability to store fat around the internal organs rather than between the skin and the muscles. And it helps to have dark skin.

Proper training will not make any man into a Mr. America unless he has the genetic potential. Few people have this potential. But proper training will improve anyone's muscular size, strength, shape, and condition. It will do so quickly. But it will not make a mediocre bodybuilder into a world champion. Champions are born more often than they are made.

18

muscular pumping

When muscles are engaged in any kind of work they demand an increased blood flow, or circulation, with its cargo of oxygen and other nutrients. Increased circulation is important for two reasons. First, it provides the muscles with the fuel it requires. Second, the flowing blood picks up and removes the larger-than-normal amount of waste that is being produced.

If the work assigned to the muscles continues for some time, the inflow of blood into the muscle and its subsequent outflow strike a happy balance. A feature of this balance is a slight enlargement of the working muscle.

However, if the muscles are worked at nearly maximum intensity, as in a heavy barbell exercise, and if the repetitions are executed consecutively, the engorgement of the muscle produces congestion in its interior, thereby swelling the arm to a degree that is often astonishing. The process by which the arm has become engorged is called *pumping*. A pumped upper arm may gain a full half inch over its normal size.

When pumped to that extent, an arm will feel very heavy, which is not surprising, since its actual weight has temporarily been increased. It will also feel stiff, since its flexibility will be temporarily reduced. In most cases the degree of muscularity will be reduced. The muscles will look much larger and will be much larger but will appear less defined than they normally do. In a few cases, particularly in a bodybuilder with an extreme degree of muscularity, a pumped muscle may actually appear more defined.

In most forms of work the effects of pumping usually occur without being noticed. For example, few people are aware that their lower legs are usually a half inch larger at night than they are early in the morning. Their calves increase in size during the day as a result of pumping. During the night, when the calves are resting, their circulation requirements are reduced greatly, and their size is decreased.

THE EFFECTS OF PUMPING

As far as pumping is concerned, weight training exercises are similar to any other kind of exercise. The number of repetitions performed and the relative intensity of effort are the only significant factors. But, in most exercise, movements are discontinued before any great degree of pumping is produced. For this reason, many new athletes feel that weight training exercises are somehow different. When they become involved in weight training, they notice the effects of pumping for the first time.

Many new trainees are convinced that they are already becoming "muscle bound," as a result of their initial workout. In reality, muscular pumping is an indication that worthwhile efforts are being expended. If no noticeable degree of pumping is produced, then an exercise is doing little to build muscular size and strength. Although a noticeable degree of pumping becomes evident during any really productive exercise, it does not follow that an extreme degree of pumping is a sign of doing proper exercise. Actually, it is possible to produce an extreme amount of pump from exercises that do nothing to build either size or strength.

Light movements performed in sets of very high repetitions, especially if the movements are restricted in range, will produce muscular pumping without building size or strength. On the other hand, several sets of 8 to 12 repetitions of a heavy full-range movement will produce the same degree of pumping, and they will also induce maximum growth stimulation.

PUMPING AND FUTURE GROWTH

With an upper arm measurement of 16 inches prior to a workout, a bodybuilder can probably pump his arm to a measurement of 16½ inches during a hard routine. But if it is measured two hours later, his arm will be somewhat smaller, probably about 15⅞ inches. Measured 24 hours later, his arm wil be back to its normal measurement of 16 inches, or slightly larger, if growth resulted from the workout.

Accurate measurements of various body parts will show

One set of properly performed curls on a Nautilus biceps machine will quickly pump the upper arms.

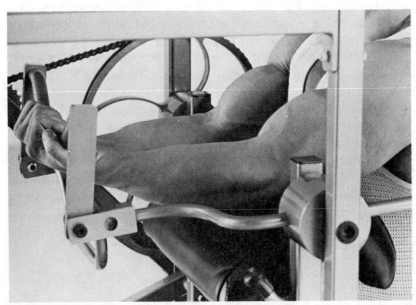

The pumped arm of Casey Viator. (Photo by Ellington Darden)

that they vary in size during an average day, even when you are not training. For example, your upper arms are slightly larger than normal when you first get out of bed in the morning and slightly smaller for an hour or so after you eat a large meal. Temperature will also affect your measurements, your arms being a bit smaller on cold days and larger on hot days.

Measurements for record-keeping purposes always should be taken under precisely identical conditions. In practice, this is difficult. For that reason, pumped measurements are useful because conditions are usually the same at the end of each workout. Furthermore, as long as your program remains unchanged, your pumped measurements will give an advance indication of your future development. If your upper arm normally pumps one half inch during a workout, and then abruptly shows a gain of three-quarters of an inch as a result of one session of the same type of workout, your arm is ready to grow during the next 48 hours.

The ability to pump a muscle to a particular size usually precedes the actual growth of that muscle to the same size as its earlier pumped-up measurement. Saying it another way, if you pump your muscle until it is larger than is normal at the end of a regular workout, you can be assured that your muscle has the solid capacity to increase in size until it is as large as it was when you first pumped it up to its new dimension.

Meanwhile, Back at Gold's Gym

Let me tell you about something I witnessed at Gold's Gym in 1980. I was visiting California and met Mike Mentzer for a workout one afternoon. Mike was about to do the arm cross on the Nautilus double chest machine. Nearby, a young bodybuilder was doing set after set of pulley cross-overs from overhead cables. The young body-builder pumped his pectorals with over 15 sets of cross-overs with a light weight which didn't seem to tax his strength. By the fifteenth set, his pectorals were red and swollen.

When Mike proceeded with *slow* arm crosses on the double chest machine with the *whole weight stack,* the young bodybuilder looked on in total amazement. Mike ground out 10 repetitions and failed on the eleventh. His face was flushed, his heart was racing, and his chest looked huge.

After staring for a full minute in complete disbelief, the young bodybuilder returned to his cables and proceeded to work his chest in the same low-intensity, non-productive manner.

Some of us will never learn!

—Roger Schwab
Director, Main Line Nautilus
Bryn Mawr, Pennsylvania
From a letter to Ellington Darden

19

layoffs and plateaus

Training should never be permitted to degenerate into a rut. If you merely go through the motions without extending yourself, boredom is bound to plague you. If you become bored, your training will not produce worthwhile results, and if this continues long enough, you may lose interest in exercise of any kind.

Best results are produced if layoffs are occasionally permitted, as long as they are not scheduled in advance. If you look forward to a scheduled layoff, your incentive is diminished. If you are forced to take an unexpected layoff, you will return to training with new enthusiasm.

Apart from psychological considerations, it is true that the body requires such breaks. A proper layoff should involve at least a week of inactivity. In some cases one solid month away from training will do more good than six months of steady training.

If any degree of muscular size or strength is lost, it will be reestablished within a short time period. In most cases progress toward unprecedented levels of ability will follow.

In fact, a best performance in many types of sports can only be produced *after* a layoff. Power lifters, for example, are well advised to avoid training entirely for several days prior to a contest. While a longer layoff might result in a reduced performance, a few days out of training often make it possible to lift more than ever before. Similar results can be observed in those sports activities that require brief, but very intense effort: pole vaulting, shot putting, and sprinting are examples.

TEN DAYS OF NO TRAINING

In almost all cases, if one month of constant training fails to produce marked improvement, the need for a layoff is indicated. Again, the layoff should last at least a full week. Ten days would be better yet, since training could normally be terminated on a Friday and resumed on Monday of the second following week. Two weekends of rest can sometimes do wonders for a bodybuilder's progress.

Individuals differ in their reactions to exercise after a layoff, but in most cases training should be resumed at the same level at which it was terminated.

Except in cases involving injuries or illnesses, layoffs from training should never exceed a period of one month. Within 30 days, all normal physiological requirements for a break in training will surely have been met. Too many breaks in training will reduce a trainee's level of ability without compensation.

PLATEAUS

As a result of training, progress should be both steady and rapid, as it will be if the guidelines offered in this book are understood and followed. Viewed on a month-to-month basis, occasional sticking points or plateaus will probably be encountered. In most cases, a plateau is a direct result of

Advanced bodybuilders such as Casey Viator should be required to take an unscheduled ten-day layoff from high-intensity training at least once every nine to twelve months. (Photo by Ellington Darden)

overtraining, which can be overcome by a brief layoff. In some cases, another remedy must be found.

On encountering a stubborn sticking point, many bodybuilders eventually assume that they have reached their individual potential. Almost always, they are wrong. The potential levels of attainment are so high that few individuals ever approach them.

When a plateau is experienced that will not respond to a brief layoff, or when a plateau is encountered immediately following a layoff, then one of two possible methods probably will end it. If your strength has not already reached a level at which additional resistance would be unwise because of safety considerations, resistance should be markedly increased. For example, if you are stuck on 10 repetitions in the curl, with a resistance of 100 pounds, the weight should be increased to 110 pounds. This extra weight will probably reduce your curling ability so that you can do only three or four repetitions. But if you perform all of your sets as *maximum possible sets,* you will make progress. And soon, experience indicates, you will be able to perform 10 repetitions even with the 110-pound weight.

What if your level of strength is already so high that taking on extra weight would be unwise because of the threat of damage to your framework? Then turn to this other plateau-busting remedy: simply discontinue the unproductive exercise and find a similar one to replace it.

If none of these methods—layoffs, markedly increased resistance, or substitution of a similar exercise—produces the desired result, overtraining should be suspected. But do not take a layoff—at least not yet. If 12 exercises are being performed, try reducing the number to 10 and/or reducing the weekly workouts from three to two.

If results are still not forthcoming, the fault usually will be due to the maturity factor. In other words, you simply may be too young. For example, trainees between the ages of 25 and 35 usually get better results than those between the ages of 15 and 25.

Total failure to produce continuing progress is almost never encountered. When it is, you are probably suffering from an undetected illness or failing to devote the proper intensity of effort to your workouts.

20

nutrition

Thirty years ago the subject of nutrition was seldom mentioned in muscle-building publications. In the early 1950s the supposed benefit gained from massive amounts of protein was announced, and the floodgates were opened. Since then, nutrition propaganda has reached such proportions that it dominates the field of physical training.

Years ago trainees who bought a barbell automatically became former customers; a barbell lasts forever, so there is no such thing as a continuing customer. In addition, the market size was limited and no great profits were made by anybody. A can of protein powder, however, does not last forever. If a barbell fails to live up to advertised claims, its shortcoming is usually obvious to the user. The average bodybuilder, however, cannot judge the value of a food supplement.

Since many celebrated bodybuilders are willing to endorse nutritional supplements for money, it is not difficult for advertisers to purchase glowing reports of outstanding results produced by using their products. It is interesting to note that most such advertisements employ the same few people over and over. Their case histories are always reported after the fact, never *while* they are making the claimed progress with the product. Supposedly using the advertised products, they are always outstanding examples of muscular development. That they use a certain item is never mentioned until after the individuals involved have become well-known figures.

A few weeks prior to the 1971 Mr. America contest, for example, a California manufacturer of food supplements sent Casey Viator a contract offering him $1,000 worth of products. In return he wanted the unrestricted use of Casey's pictures and endorsements to publicize his supplements. If this offer had been accepted, which it was not, bodybuilders would have been subjected to a barrage of advertising giving the California products full credit for Casey's success. Casey had never used any of those products.

NUTRITION'S PLACE IN MUSCLE BUILDING

It should be understood that the quantity of food bodybuilders eat is of far more importance than the type of food they eat. For years several bodybuilders have publicized the fact that building muscle is 80% diet and nutrition. Of such testimony Arthur Jones says, "Instead of being 80%, bodybuilding is 100% nutrition—but only if you don't eat. Just try going without food for a week and see what happens to your body!"

The truth is this: *nutrition accounts for less than 5% of the muscle development process.* In building muscular size and strength, proper exercise and rest are far more important than diet and nutrition.

Over the last 30 years, no advice has proved superior to the National Research Council's recommendation: eat a well-balanced diet composed of daily servings of the basic four food groups—meat, dairy products, fruits and vegetables, and breads and cereals. Nutritional experts who have broken down a bodybuilder's need further say that the ideal diet is composed of 59% carbohydrates, 28% fats, and 13% proteins.

DEEMPHASIZING PROTEIN

These facts about nutrition are not at all what the muscle-building magazines want bodybuilders to believe. Most of them report that "muscles are made up of protein" and "to build large muscles, you need massive amounts of protein."

The physiological fact is that muscles are composed mostly of water. More than 70% of a muscle is water, and only 22% is protein. Rarely is an American athlete deficient in protein. In fact, research shows just the opposite. It also shows that athletes, especially bodybuilders and weightlifters, consume three times as much protein per day as they need for maximum muscular growth.

How much protein per day does a trainee need? Here is a guideline: Multiply body weight in pounds by .36 grams. If

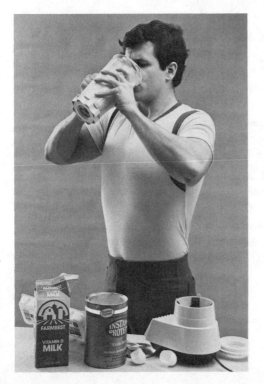

Bodybuilders should not be misled by food supplement advertising that says you need to add protein supplements to your diet for larger muscles. Building larger muscles is much more dependent on proper exercise and adequate rest than on diet and nutrition.

you weigh 200 pounds, you will require only 72 grams daily. Even a 300-pound bodybuilder, if such a creature exists, would need no more than 108 grams daily. Yet, the consumption of more than 300 grams of protein per day has become an important ritual for most bodybuilders. Such unscientific eating practices are unnecessary as well as potentially dangerous.

EXCESSIVE PROTEIN DANGER

Consuming massive amounts of protein is primarily threatening to the liver and kidneys. These are important organs in the protein utilization process. Since protein cannot be stored to any extent in the body, the metabolism and excretion of nonstorable protein loads can impose serious stresses and may cause a disastrous enlargement of two very important organs.

Once again, it must be emphasized that massive amounts of protein foods or any type of protein supplements are not needed for bodybuilding purposes. At best, surplus protein will increase a bodybuilder's fatty tissue. At worst, it will play havoc with his liver and kidneys.

Large amounts of vitamins and minerals are also counterproductive for bodybuilders. Vitamins and minerals are certainly important to your health, fitness, and muscle building. But nutritional scientists are quick to point out that all necessary nutrients are easily available in a reasonably well-balanced diet. Vitamin and mineral pills simply increase the nutritional value of a user's urine and feces. Massive amounts of almost any vitamin or mineral can damage important organs and tissues.

For a thorough discussion of diet, nutrition, and muscular fitness, obtain a copy of *The Nautilus Nutrition Book*, published by Contemporary Books in 1981.

In the final analysis, the subject of nutrition for muscle building probably is the most completely understood factor

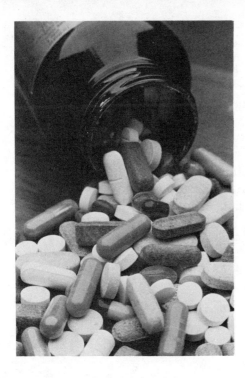

A bodybuilder who regularly consumes a reasonably balanced diet does *not* need to take vitamin and mineral pills.

The basis of good nutrition for developing the body is eating a variety of foods from the basic four food groups.

involved in physical training. Unfortunately, this understanding is not shared by most bodybuilders. Many have been
brainwashed into spending thousands of dollars on products
of little or no value.

All that is needed for building muscle from a nutritional
viewpoint is the daily consumption of an unglamorous,
reasonably well-balanced diet. Every bit of this unglamorous
food can be purchased at the local grocery store or super-
market.

21

anabolic steroid drugs

There is no known drug that will improve the performance of a healthy individual . . . and there never will be
such a drug; normal health being just that, normal . . .
superhealth, by definition, being impossible.

—Arthur Jones

The most popular drugs currently used by bodybuilders
are the androgenic-anabolic steroids. *Androgenic* refers to
the production of masculine characteristics, while *anabolic*
relates to the conversion of food within a cell. These drugs
are synthetic forms of testosterone and other male hormones. A few of the most common brand names are
Dianabol, Winstrol, Anavar, Nilevar, Durabolin, and Methyl-
testosterone.

When steroid drugs became available for experimental
and therapeutic use in the 1930s, scientists used them to
help maintain strength in aging men. During World War II
they were used to help restore positive nitrogen balance in
victims of forced starvation.

In 1960, a Pennsylvania physician who was interested in
weight training began to experiment on himself. He rea-

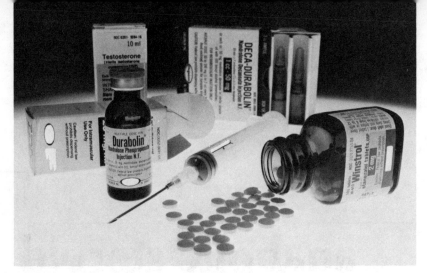

Anabolic steroid drugs are fool's gold.

soned that if anabolic steroids reversed negative nitrogen balance, they would somehow increase the utilization of protein to form additional muscle in those who trained their bodies and were well nourished. At first he used an injectable steroid; and later he used an oral one. After a while he was satisfied that he had increased his muscular size and strength at a greater rate than if he had only lifted weights and eaten heartily. Reporting his observations in a weight training magazine, he started the craze for the use of these drugs.

Within a short time football players, shot-putters, and other athletes picked up the idea from bodybuilders and weightlifters. Because androgenic-anabolic steroids were controlled drugs in the United States, physicians were soon overwhelmed with requests for prescriptions. Many of them wrote them willingly at first. Then the serious side effects, which we will discuss later, began to appear. Touring athletes later found they could buy the drugs over the counter, without prescriptions, in Mexico and other foreign countries.

This abuse, even with serious side effects and other dangers, is still the rule in the competitive bodybuilding world. The fact is that massive amounts of steroids are being consumed all over the world by bodybuilders without a shred of solid evidence of any positive results.

THE TRUTH ABOUT STEROIDS

An up-to-date review of research on the effects of androgenic-anabolic steroids on male athletes was written in 1980 by Dr. Allan J. Ryan, editor of the *Physician and Sportsmedicine*. Dr. Ryan critically reviewed 25 studies that dealt with the administration of anabolic steroids for increasing muscular strength. Twelve of the 25 studies recorded some improvements in strength, while 13 did not.

Dr. Ryan found a long list of inconsistencies among the studies that claimed strength improvement. For example, only one study used lean body mass as a measure of muscular improvement; the others used gross body weight. Only four of the 12 studies used double-blind techniques, where neither the administrator nor the athlete himself knew whether he was receiving the real drug or a placebo. No attempts were made in any of the studies to learn about or control the subjects' diets. The number of subjects was not very large. Poor experimental designs characterized most of the reports. Errors of calculation were found in three studies, which had a significant bearing on the claimed results.

On the other hand, Dr. Ryan judged that the 13 studies that failed to find significant improvements in strength were consistent in their conclusions and similar in their methods. Ten of the 13 studies were double blind. The number of subjects in them was greater, and the experimental periods lasted 50% longer. Serious attempts were made to determine the composition of subjects' diets in two of the studies. In all 13 studies, the designs of the experiments were judged to be sound. No mistakes were observable in the calculations as reported. And no conclusions were drawn that were not justified by the methods employed and the data obtained.

In the final analysis, Dr. Ryan noted that, in spite of the claims made by some that the use of anabolic steriods in conjunction with progressive weight training produces a greater increase in muscular size and strength than weight training alone, *there was no substantial evidence that this was so.* On the contrary, there is evidence that will bear close scrutiny that anabolic steroids will *not* contribute significantly to gains in muscular size and strength in healthy adult males. Furthermore, it is probable that the presumed increase of muscle tissue was on account of the action of anabolic steroids causing the body to retain salt and water. In short, those subjects had not added any muscle mass whatever. They had merely become waterlogged.

THAT PUFFY LOOK

When a bodybuilder takes steriods for a while he often gains body weight. He does not know that this is almost certainly the result of water retention. So he assumes that his muscles are really getting bigger.

"He's got that puffy look," is a phrase used by body-builders to describe athletes who are consuming drugs. To those who understand, it is obvious that a puffy look on the face, neck, and lower body is a characteristic of water retention. Any increase in muscular size and strength is anything but puffy looking.

Some bodybuilders do increase their muscular size and strength while consuming steriods. But this increase, instead of being caused by steroids, is a result of training harder combined with the placebo effect.

THE PLACEBO EFFECT

The term *placebo* comes from the Latin word meaning "I will please." A standard dictionary definition is "a preparation containing no medicine but given for its psychological effect." Often, the placebo effect is achieved with such substances as sugar pills or injections of sterile water.

The placebo effect, however, includes more than the use of substances. It is used to cover such nonspecific aspects of treatment as the bodybuilder's beliefs and expectations, the physician's or supervisor's beliefs and expectations, and the psychological interaction between the two.

As a rule, the bodybuilder who is injected with an anabolic steroid trains harder and notices a gradual increase in the size of his arms. The runner who takes protein pills and then sprints the fastest 100-meter dash of his life gives credit to his pills. The basketball coach whose team is on a winning streak wears the same coat and tie to every game. All of these people are being fooled by the placebo effect.

The problem in bodybuilding is not with the placebo effect itself, but with the people who misunderstand its power and do not give credit where it is due. The bodybuilder who takes drugs relies on the placebo effect without realizing it. Thus, he believes he knows what he is doing. In so doing, he is encouraging himself to form a habit of using things he does not need. And a successful bodybuilder, by professing his faith in steroids, may be encouraging other trainees to emulate his habits, to believe in steroid drugs as he does.

Studies show that a placebo will produce an effect in about 50% of all patients. Other studies demonstrate that placebos tend to be more effective when given in higher dosages, when taken by injection, when unpleasant in taste, or when administered as pills in certain colors or shapes.

SIDE EFFECTS OF STEROIDS

Although steroid drugs are real medicine, what they were clinically designed to do and what they actually do in the athlete's mind are worlds apart. Clinically, androgenic-anabolic steroids are used to treat some anemias, osteoporosis of the bone, chronic debilitating illness, and male hormone deficiencies. Steroids were not designed to make healthy bodybuilders bigger or stronger.

The fact that steroid drugs do not offer any chemical benefit to bodybuilders would be relatively insignificant if there were no harmful side effects. A New York physician recently examined more than 300 athletes who were consuming large amounts of steroid drugs. He stated emphatically that he detected clinical damage in 100% of the athletes up to six months after they had discontinued taking them. He found permanent damage in more than 25%. These side effects included testicular atrophy, pituitary inhibition, enlarged prostate, fluid retention (high blood pressure), kidney damage (hardening of the kidney arteries), and impaired liver function (fibrosis).

In women, steroids can produce a deepened voice, growth of facial and chest hair, liver damage, clitoral enlargement, menstrual irregularities, and impairment of reproductive capacity.

WHAT CAN BE DONE

Anabolic steroids have been banned from amateur sports for years. Urine tests to detect them were developed in 1973 and are now used in many international competitions. Some athletes, including several Olympic weightlifters, have been disqualified because of steroid traces discovered in their urine.

Testing for drugs, however, has yet to be introduced to bodybuilding contests. One reason may be that an athlete can stop taking steroids a few weeks before competing and usually avoid detection.

So far, neither legislation nor threats of permanent disqualification has been effective in stopping steroid use. Testing is expensive, relatively unproductive, and supports the idea that athletes may gain an advantage by using drugs. Apparently, the only hope for banishing this practice is to establish an accelerated program of education for bodybuilders, weightlifters, and all other athletes.

Truly, anabolic steroids are fool's gold.

22

women and bodybuilding

"BUT I DON'T WANT LARGE MUSCLES"

After observing several dozen women pose in a national bodybuilding championship, one woman in the audience was overheard saying, "I'd really like to exercise, but I don't want large, well-defined muscles like those women onstage have."

The truth is that she probably could not have developed large muscles if she wanted to. Very few women have the appropriate genetic potential, long muscle bellies, and adequate supplies of male hormones to build large, well-defined muscles over their bodies. Generally speaking, 99.9999% of American women cannot develop large muscles under any circumstances.

The 25 women who compete annually in the National Bodybuilding Championships for Women have much rarer

The women who compete in bodybuilding contests have rarer inherited physical characteristics that do men who compete in bodybuilding contests. (Photo by John Balik)

inherited characteristics than do the 100 men who compete in the same event for men. Given that the desired result is to build large well-defined muscles with a low percentage of body fat, only one woman out of approximately a million has this potential. And, at least in 1981, it seems that the trend in women's bodybuilding is to judge a contest along lines similar to those used in men's contests. If this is the case, and it seems to be, then people connected with women's bodybuilding are distorting well-established physiological facts.

PHYSIOLOGICAL FACTS

First, it is impossible to build a large muscle unless the woman trainee has long muscle bellies and short tendon attachments. This factor was discussed in detail in Chapter

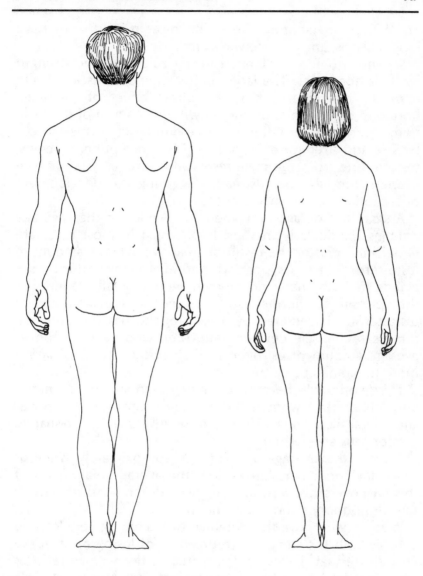

Basic body shape comparisons between the average American man and woman reveal that women have wider hips and narrower shoulders than do men. Women also store twice as much subcutaneous fat over their hips and thighs.

17. Without belaboring the point, most men do not have long muscles, and even fewer women do.

Second, women are limited in muscular size and strength by their hormones. The larger better-defined muscle mass in men is no accident; it is the direct effect of the male hormone testosterone on the growth mechanism of the male body. Before puberty there is little difference in the muscular size and strength of boys and girls. Once puberty begins, testosterone from the male testes and estrogen from female ovaries enter the bloodstream, triggering the development of secondary sexual characteristics.

A small percentage of women do have larger-than-average muscles, particularly in their legs, which in most cases are either inherited or the result of an above-average amount of testosterone in the system. The adrenal glands and the sex glands in both men and women secrete small amounts of the opposite sex hormones. If a larger-than-usual amount of testosterone is secreted by a female, she has the potential for greater muscle development. Men who have an above-average amount of estrogen in their systems tend to have a more feminine appearance.

Third, primarily because of their potential for pregnancy and childbirth, women have wider hips and narrower shoulders than men. This is a disadvantage if V-shaped proportions are desired.

Fourth, the average woman has approximately twice as much fat under her skin as does the average man. Most of this fat covers her hips and thighs and is related directly to female hormones and motherhood.

Women who have the potential of becoming very lean do so only with the unattractive prospect of losing most of the fatty tissue that makes up their breasts. If a woman reduces her body fat below 8% of her weight, her menstrual cycle may become sporadic or cease. The long-term effects of having no monthly period are not known, but most women who cease menstruation seem to suffer more from psychological than from physiological problems.

PROPER EXERCISE BENEFITS WOMEN MORE THAN MEN

If women's bodybuilding is to succeed, it must be based and judged on criteria centered around the perfection of the physiological characteristics of women, not men. In many respects, women have more to gain from proper training than do men. This is true because most women have neglected the strength of their muscles for much of their lives. It is never too late. *Not only will proper exercise increase a woman's strength, but it will improve significantly her muscle tone, flexibility, heart-lung endurance, and overall appearance.*

Regardless of whether an interested woman wants to enter a bodybuilding contest or improve other aspects of her physical fitness, the guidelines for men presented in this book apply with almost equal validity to women.

23

the ultimate physique

The ultimate physique has been discussed for many years. Which contributes most, heritage or training? Physicians and scientists have debated this subject—and so has Arthur Jones.

While visiting the Nautilus headquarters in Florida, a former Mr. America told Jones that he was one of two surviving triplets and that his brother actually has the better calves, though the brother has never trained with weights. Later Jones saw the brothers together, and the untrained man's calves *were* superior. This proved to Jones that the rigorous training to which the former Mr. America had devoted so many years had served only to reduce the size of his outstanding calves. Their size and shape were the result of heredity and probably they would have been even better if he had never trained them.

Later, on hearing that Jones had mentioned this fact in an article for *Iron Man* magazine, this bodybuilder lodged a complaint, demanding that this fact not be published. Why? Apparently he intended to give the credit for his calf development to a machine he planned to promote.

This anecdote illustrates that much of the bodybuilder's potential depends on heredity. Some people, like the man mentioned above, will enjoy outstanding development of at least some body parts without ever training. Some people will never reach an equal degree of development regardless of how hard they train or what they eat. But most people can achieve muscular size and strength that is beyond anything they might believe. And given good heredity, a few men can reach a level of size and strength that is almost unbelievable.

Since most bodybuilders are interested in reaching their own particular limits of muscular size, the following points should be of interest.

THE TWENTY-INCH ARM

To begin this discussion bluntly, most of the measurements claimed by top bodybuilders are simply untrue. The largest muscular arm that Arthur Jones ever measured was Sergio Oliva's, which, measured accurately when "cold," was $20\frac{1}{8}$ inches. Arnold Schwarzenegger's arm was $19\frac{7}{8}$ inches when pumped slightly—probably $19\frac{1}{2}$ inches cold. Bill Pearl's largest arm, his left arm, was $18\frac{5}{8}$ inches when he was at a body weight of 222 in 1960. At the 1971 NABBA Mr. Universe contest in London, Pearl's publicized arm size was listed as $20\frac{1}{4}$ inches. It was evident to Jones that Pearl's arms were actually smaller than when he measured them 11 years earlier. When Pearl and Oliva stood side by side it was obvious that Sergio's arms literally dwarfed Bill's. Sergio's arms actually measured $20\frac{1}{8}$ inches at that time.

Casey Viator's arms were $19\frac{5}{16}$ at their largest when he was training in Florida—and were $18\frac{1}{16}$ when he first came to Lake Helen in 1970.

Certain factors affect the appearance of a man's arms: the size of his head, and the length and shape of his arms. An

The 20⅛-inch upper arm and 15½-inch forearm of Sergio Oliva. (Photo by Inge Cook)

arm might measure 17 inches and look quite large, or measure 18 inches and appear to be only a little above average size. In fact, an arm that measures 18 inches is enormous, a 19-inch arm is really huge, and a 20-inch arm defies belief. Claiming 20-inch arms, or even larger measurements, is common today. In his lifetime, Arthur Jones has measured only *one* 20-inch arm. While he hasn't measured the arms of everybody on the bodybuilding scene, he has seen all of the better-known bodybuilders standing next to some of the men that he has measured. The arms of Oliva and Schwarzenegger literally dwarf the arms of every other man he has seen. In peak condition, Lou Ferrigno probably has arms that measure over 20 inches. But because of his height, weight, and overall body size, his arms do not appear as big as do Oliva's and Schwarzenegger's.

It is interesting that in many cases an arm's mass will be quite large, whereas it will measure less than expected. If the biceps and triceps are longer than normal, then the bulk of muscle may be far out of proportion with the measurement. The same thing is true of forearms. Both Casey Viator and Sergio Oliva have very long forearm muscles. While both of these men have larger-than-average forearm measurements, the mass of their forearm muscles is much greater than the measurements might indicate. Casey's forearms are nearly 15½ inches when "cold," at right angles to the bone.

This photograph of Casey Viator was taken in May of 1978. He weighed 223 pounds. Notice the fullness in his upper arms and forearms. (Photo by Inge Cook)

Sergio's forearms are a bit over 15½ inches. By comparison, Bill Pearl's larger forearm was 13¾ inches.

Sergio Oliva's biceps muscles are so long that he has much less than the normal range of movement around the axis of his elbow—approximately 120 degrees of rotary movement as opposed to 160 degrees in the average man. Sergio cannot bend his arms as far as most men. This has little to do with his degree of development but is a result of much-longer-than-average biceps muscles. Arnold Schwarzenegger's arm, almost as large as Sergio's, shows no signs of restricted movement around the elbow joint. Furthermore, since the greatest thickness of Sergio's forearms occurs near the middle of his forearms, his movement is further restricted. Instead of fitting into the normal hollow of the biceps just above the elbow, the mass of his forearms meets the middle of his biceps.

LARGER THAN THEY MEASURE

Sergio's arms, therefore, are actually larger than they measure. The mass of muscle is far greater than measurement would indicate, which is a result of heredity and not a result of training. While his training produced his muscular size, his heredity made it possible.

His limited range of movement, however, prevents Sergio from fully contracting his biceps into the high peak displayed by some bodybuilders. Sergio simply cannot bend his arms far enough to reach the required degree· of contraction. It might well be that Sergio's arms would measure more than they do if they were actually less massive—if this reduction came in the form of shorter biceps and forearm flexors.

Regardless of their measurement, Sergio's arms are so big that they must be seen to be appreciated. Some people cannot believe their eyes. In a full-length picture that Arthur Jones took of Sergio in 1971, the width of the flexed upper arms exceeded the height of Sergio's head. His arms were literally larger than his head, a size ratio never before approached by anyone.

Jones says that Sergio represents the closest thing to an ultimate physique that he has seen. Is Sergio's, then, the

How big is Sergio's arm? Look carefully at the photo. Sergio's arm is actually wider than his head is high—the width of his arm exceeds the distance from below his chin to above the top of his head. No bodybuilder in history has ever had an arm that large. (Photo by Inge Cook)

At a height of five feet, ten inches, Sergio Oliva weighed 233 pounds when this photograph was taken. (Photo by Inge Cook)

ultimate physique? For most bodybuilders, it is far beyond the limit permitted by individual potential. But it is almost certain that somebody will eventually exceed even Sergio's present size and proportions. Until someone actually matches him, however, he certainly does represent the ultimate physique.

A REALISTIC GOAL

Exercise is a requirement for normal health. Yet, in the opinion of the average person, the results produced by weight training are somehow different from the muscular size and strength that come from regular work. Thus we commonly hear the terms *real strength*, and *natural strength*.

The size and strength produced by training are looked upon as temporary, useless, or even dangerous.

Such opinions are usually the result of jealousy, perhaps brought into the open because outstanding muscular size, unlike intelligence or wealth, cannot be hidden from view. Comic strip heroes are almost invariably given the physiques of advanced bodybuilders, but their development is presented as natural. Supposedly, they grew naturally to such proportions. Had they been required to train in order to build their size, their image would somehow be lessened in the public's mind.

Because of this attitude, most advanced bodybuilders find themselves living apart, confined to the company of other bodybuilders and people attracted to bodybuilders. In our society, we are faced with this conflict: Most people are encouraged to stand out, and then considered freaks if they do. It is almost impossible, in fact, for the average person to stand out in any way. Being able to handle such uniqueness depends in great part on your desires—how much attention you want or can stand—as well as on your ability to view things in a practical light. Arthur Jones frequently compares bodybuilders to Mark Twain's "two-headed stranger": Upon seeing him, one boy remarked that he wouldn't want to be like that. Another boy, however, viewed the possibilities more practically, saying, "Oh, that would be dandy—eat for two but only stub toes for one." Most advanced body-builders do everything they can to call attention to their size and then seem to be surprised by the reactions they produce.

In general, unusual muscular size will not attract favorable attention. If your well-being depends on the opinion of others, attracting attention because of your physique will usually hurt you far more than it will help you. In the public's mind, a man with an outstanding physique has nothing else. This, of course, is outright stupidity, but it can still hurt you if you are unaware of it.

Attracting favorable attention, untainted by jealousy, seems to be rare. So, in the end, it comes down to what a trainee seeks or can take. But all bodybuilders should remember that the price of attracting attention as a result of a muscular physique is always high.

The only question that seems to be important to most trainees involves how much muscular size and strength an individual can build. The answer is that it does not appear that anybody has ever reached his limit. What is strange is that most bodybuilders prevent themselves from nearing their limits of muscular size by persistently overtraining. In any case, almost without regard for starting condition, size of bones, length of muscles, or even age, you should be able to build a level of muscular size and strength that will amaze most people. A few individuals can attain a muscular size

The photograph below shows the dramatic difference between an eighteen-inch and a fourteen-inch upper arm. Due to only average length biceps and triceps muscles, the man on the right should have a realistic goal of only a sixteen-inch arm. (Photo by Inge Cook)

that would amaze anybody. But it now seems clear that quickly reaching such a degree of development requires a very small amount of training—and please note the word *requires*, since it should be understood that more training will literally prevent better final results.

Eventually, somebody with outstanding potential will start training properly right from the start of his career. And two or three years later we will see an example of muscular size far beyond anything yet produced. Will such size be attractive? To the average person, certainly not. Will it be desirable? That is a matter of individual taste. But such an example will at least be valuable for scientific purposes, as an example of what can be done.

"If an advanced bodybuilder had suddenly appeared on the scene 400 years ago," writes Jones, "he would probably have been burned at the stake. If you have the potential for unusual muscular size, and if you actually build such size to a maximum possible degree, you will undoubtedly be looked upon as an outright freak.

"In my opinion," Jones continues, "a realistic goal is far better."

24

the present state of the art

Someone once said, "Nothing can stop an idea whose time has come." And the time has certainly come for improvements in bodybuilding methods and systems of training, tools, and the use of those tools.

The Nautilus machines are not the only new development on the scene. A number of people are working on new concepts. Each new development has its own supporters, and, according to those supporters each new development is the best.

It would be wrong to assume that only new tools are good. The barbell is a good tool, one that is capable of producing outstanding muscular development. But it is not a perfect tool.

The main trouble, as discussed in earlier chapters, seems to stem from the fact that humans are rotary animals living on a planet that provides reciprocal, or straight, up-and-down resistance. In practice, trainees seldom encounter anything except reciprocal resistance.

UNDERSTANDING BEGINS WITH FUNCTION

"Did you ever wonder," writes Arthur Jones, "why screws are designed with a right-hand thread? Because most people are right-handed, and because right-handed people have more power for making clockwise movements than they do for making counterclockwise movements. When you are turning a tool clockwise, with your right hand, the primary function of the biceps muscle is aiding the work—and you are strongest.

"And why is your thumb located on the top of your hand instead of on the bottom?" Jones continues. "Because, located where it is, the thumb serves as an anchor for the entire hand during clockwise movements of the right hand. Try twisting your right hand hard in a counterclockwise direction and see what happens. In these cases the thumb is of little or no assistance for maintaining a grip. To be of assistance, it would have to be located at the bottom of your hand, opposing your little finger."

Before it is possible to design a rational exercise tool, it is necessary to understand exactly what the functions of human muscular structures are. It is not enough to design a tool that will simply provide resistance. A pick and shovel will provide more work than most people can stand, but will do very little in the way of building muscular size and strength.

The hand is a superb clutching tool. It is just as superior as a turning tool. The point is that no engineer, no human being, could have designed it without understanding the functions of every muscle with which it was involved. When Arthur Jones designed the Nautilus machines, he was determined that somehow they should involve every fiber of every muscle in the process of increasing size and strength.

MUSCULAR GROWTH AND RECOVERY ABILITY

Muscular size and strength occur ordinarily as a part of normal growth. Little exercise is required for reaching normal development. Bodybuilders, however, seek abnormal levels. Their objective is to build maximum levels of size and strength in the shortest period of time and as a result of the least effort. In short, they should be looking for the most productive method of exercise.

A healthy body will provide levels of size and strength according to its perception of what is needed for normal requirements, plus a bit more as a reserve for emergency use. As long as existing levels are adequate, as long as extreme demands are not made on the body, no additional size or strength will be provided. To produce growth, as both science and experience agree, demands must be made in excess of normal. Only then will the body attempt to provide the size and strength required to meet these demands if it can. Note the phrase *if it can.*

The body is a very complex factory, constantly making hundreds of delicate changes that transform food and oxygen into the many chemicals needed by the various parts of the system. In a healthy body the system works perfectly, meeting all requirements and maintaining a reserve for emergencies. But there is a limit to the chemical conversions that the body can make within a given time period. If an individual's requirements exceed that limit, his body eventually will be overworked to a point of total collapse, even to the point of death.

For example, a man can run for 10 minutes, then rest for 23 hours and 50 minutes, and then run another 10 minutes, and so on. In 23 hours and 50 minutes, the body easily recovers from a 10-minute run. Or this man can run for 30 minutes and then rest for 23 hours and 30 minutes, and recover. But he cannot run for 1 hour and then repeat such a run after only 8 hours of rest. If he tried it, he would probably collapse because he would be exceeding his recovery ability.

What happens when this man adopts a logical training program that calls for a series of daily runs of 10 minutes each, after which small increments are gradually added? If all goes according to plan, without injury or illness, his running ability also increases. At some point he will establish a set pattern and a distance to run. He will feel comfortable with it and it will fit into his life-style. Yet, no matter how many months he runs, his running ability will not improve. He has reached the point at which his daily runs exactly match his body's tolerance.

Suppose he wants to improve. He runs faster but for the same length of time. Now he becomes less comfortable. He is doing more work, but he is also committing a big mistake. To his astonishment, his runs become more painful. His spirit sags. Why? Because he has exceeded his recovery ability. If he continues, negative growth will reduce the size of his muscles.

The recovery ability of the body provides normal growth. It also provides abnormal growth, if such abnormal growth is required, and if the recovery ability is able to meet the requirements. It should be understood that it is impossible for a trainee to exhaust his recovery ability or even exceed it while doing absolutely nothing to stimulate abnormal growth. *Obviously, then, to be productive, an exercise must stimulate abnormal growth as much as possible while disturbing the recovery ability as little as possible.* Under this concept an ideal exercise would be infinitely hard and infinitely brief. It would provide maximum growth stimulation while leaving the trainee's recovery ability in the best possible shape to meet the requirements for growth.

CONTINUOUS RESISTANCE

When the barbell was invented it became more productive than previously existing exercise tools simply and only because it provided harder exercise. But a barbell still leaves a lot to be desired. While barbell exercises are harder than freehand exercises, for example, they still are not as hard as they should be.

With the relatively unimportant exceptions of wrist curls, calf raises, and a few other standard exercises, most barbell exercises work only part of the muscular structures. In most cases a barbell cannot provide resistance for all the muscles. Remember that barbells provide only reciprocal resistance, and most major movements are made in rotary fashion. In consequence a large part of most major movements is performed with no significant resistance.

Picture a large rubber band that has been stretched to twice its normal length. Imagine that this band is a stretched muscle, that it has power potential or stored power that has not been used, and that it cannot be used without reducing its length. While this comparison is not exact, it will serve to illustrate a point. As long as the rubber band remains stretched, it is impossible to use its power potential.

Muscle fibers perform work by reducing their length. If all the fibers of a particular muscle are shortened as much as possible (maximum contraction), it follows that there is also a maximum reduction of the overall length of that muscle. But muscles are attached across joints to bones, so a muscle cannot reduce its length without producing movement of the involved part of the body.

Now carry this reasoning a step further: If the maximum reduction has taken place in a muscle, then it follows that the maximum movement by the attached body part will have occurred. Thus, it becomes apparent that every fiber of a muscle cannot work unless that muscle is fully contracted and its related body part has moved through its fullest possible range.

Obviously, this is the real point: A state of full contraction is a prerequisite for the total involvement of a muscle. No other position than that of full contraction can totally involve all of that muscle's fibers in work.

While a position of full contraction is required for total work, it does not necessarily follow that such a position will produce total work. Muscle fibers do not become involved unless they are needed. Thus, it follows logically that a second prerequisite for total work is an imposed resistance heavy enough to require the involvement of every available muscle fiber.

Regardless of its weight, a barbell imposes no resistance on muscles in their fully contracted positions (besides the minor exceptions listed above).

With Nautilus machines, resistance is provided in all positions. Such resistance works a muscle from a position of full stretch to one of full contraction.

But even continuous resistance is not enough, though it is a great first step in the right direction. Since the strength of a muscle—both the input of strength and the output of strength—is not the same in all positions, the resistance must vary directly with the output of strength.

ISOKINETICS

One current approach to solving the problem of matching resistance to strength is called *isokinetics*. It involves the use of the inertia reel principle. By limiting the speed of movement, some exercise machine designers felt that maximum resistance would be provided in all positions. The approach worked fairly well in theory, but not in practice.

With isokinetics, there is no actual resistance. Instead, even a very small effort will move the resistance arm or bar. But the bar will only move at a certain speed, regardless of how hard you push or pull. In theory, then, if you pull as hard as possible in all positions throughout the movement, the resistance will always be right, will always be maximum resistance in any and all positions. An obvious shortcoming of the system, however, is that you are limited to a particular speed of movement. You can set this speed at almost any rate you like, but once it is set it becomes constant throughout the movement. The people who are producing such devices, of course, point directly to this actual shortcoming as one of its major advantages.

Another shortcoming is the fact that the resistance provided by this system is not omnidirectional. In effect, the trainee still has no resistance at the end of a movement. He has none in the fully contracted position, which is the only position at which all of a muscular structure can be involved.

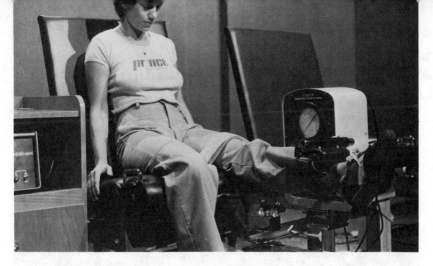

Isokinetic machines are severely limited in the muscle-building process. They do not provide stretching for flexibility, prestretching for high-intensity contraction, or negative work for greater muscle fiber involvement. (Photo by Ellington Darden)

Finally, no negative work is provided by isokinetics. In a biceps curl, for example, you can only curl upward, and once you have reached the top, you have no resistance for the downward movement.

Nautilus Sports/Medical Industries easily could have incorporated the idea of isokinetics into its machines, but the idea was rejected. Careful tests of restricted speed resistance indicated that it was vastly inferior to a resistance that could be moved at any speed.

Also, since even a small amount of effort while using an isokinetic device will produce the same speed of movement that a maximum effort would have done, you are always tempted to do less than you should. Actually, you can work at a reduced level without even being aware of it. In short, the use of isokinetics is not an efficient way to build muscular size and strength.

THE NAUTILUS ADVANTAGE

Normal training movements involve several actions: raising weight, lowering weight, accelerating weight, decelerating weight, supporting weight. All these motions, except supporting weight, can be done at any speed within a wide range from almost imperceptible movement to movement

The design of a Nautilus machine is dictated by the physiological function of a given muscle group. Here, neck and shoulder machines are being assembled in the Independence, Virginia, manufacturing plant.

that is too fast to follow. And they are all served efficiently by Nautilus machines.

Nautilus machines usually make an untrained subject sore if he uses the equipment to exhaustion during his first few workouts. This soreness may be or may not be a disadvantage. But Nautilus machines will stimulate muscle growth to a greater degree than any other device. It will do so with only a limited amount of training so that the recovery system of the body is not exhausted to the point at which growth becomes impossible.

Thus, at the moment, Nautilus equipment represents the state of the art. If you do not have access to Nautilus equipment, you should use a barbell. If and when *anything* else comes along that will improve bodybuilding productivity, it will be incorporated into Nautilus equipment.

II.

HOW TO USE NAUTILUS EQUIPMENT

the superiority of nautilus machines

Why the name *Nautilus*? According to the dictionary, a nautilus is a type of mollusk with a smooth, spiral, chambered shell. The spiral pulleys, or cams, that Arthur Jones originally used to provide variable resistance on his machines resembled a cross-section of the nautilus shell. Thus, Jones thought *Nautilus* was the perfect name for his new machines.

Nautilus machines are unique in the exercise world for a number of reasons:

1. Anyone who has used a barbell is aware that the exercises done with barbells are not full-range movements. At some point in most barbell exercises there is no effective resistance—at the start of a curl, at the end of a curl, and at the top position in a squat or a press of any kind. If you can lock out under the weight in any position, you do not have full-range resistance. In such a case you are providing exercise for only part of the muscles you are trying to work.

Full-range resistance can be provided only by a machine that rotates on a common axis with the body part that is moved by the muscles being worked. A rotational form of resistance must be provided, and it must rotate in the proper plane. When this requirement is met, it becomes possible to provide a type of exercise that is full range and that actually exceeds the normal range of movement possible for most trainees.

2. Barbells and other standard types of equipment provide resistance in one direction only—unidirectional resistance. Since the working body parts rotate, it is impossible to provide more than a small range of direct resistance. In many conventional exercises there is no direct resistance at all.

Since the direction of movement of the involved body parts is constantly changing, the direction of resistance must change in exact accord, automatically and simultaneously. Again, this requirement is provided only by a rotary form of resistance.

When the body axis of rotation that is involved in the exercise is rotating exactly in line with the axis of the rotary resistance, then omnidirectional resistance is provided. If your hand, for example, is moving straight up, then the resistance is straight down. If your hand is moving directly toward the east, then the resistance is exerting its force directly toward the west. This resistance always opposes your direction of movement by 180 degrees. The resistance is always trying to do exactly the opposite of what you are trying to do.

Your car may weigh 4,000 pounds, and you may be able to push it forward on level ground. But that does not mean that you are capable of lifting such a weight. With omnidirectional resistance, you are always lifting the weight regardless of the direction in which you may be exerting force. If your hands are going up, the weight is also going up. If your hands are going down, the weight is still going up. If your hands are going in a horizontal direction, the weight is being moved up. No matter what you do, as long as you are producing power for the purpose of causing a body part movement from a position of extension in the direction of a position of flexion, you are raising the weight.

This should make it clear that incorporating a rotary form of resistance into an exercise machine provides a number of valuable characteristics: full-range resistance, direct resistance, and omnidirectional resistance.

3. Barbells do not provide proper variation of resistance. Because of certain basic laws of physics, some variation of resistance will be encountered in most barbell exercises. For example, in a curl with a barbell, there is no resistance at the start of the movement, because the horizontal distance between the elbow and the barbell (moment arm) is zero in that position. After the first 90 degrees of movement the horizontal distance has reached its maximum point, and the resistance will feel as high as it becomes during that exercise. Later, as the movement is completed, the horizontal distance returns to zero, and again there is no effective resistance.

In that sense barbells do provide variations in resistance. But this variation is random and does more to downgrade the exercises than to improve them. Because of random variation, you will encounter sticking points, places where the weight seems far heavier than it does in other places, and points where there is no effective resistance at all.

Muscles are stronger in some positions than in other positions. In general, muscles are strongest when fully contracted. Because of the way in which they function, the only position that will involve all the fibers is one of full contraction. In almost all barbell exercises no resistance is working against the involved muscles in the position of full contraction. An unavoidable result in barbell exercises, therefore, is that muscles are worked only in their weakest positions and are not worked at all in their strongest positions.

With the Nautilus machines, required variations in resistance are properly provided; the resistance changes throughout the movements. In general, resistance is lowest at the start of the movement; it increases as it progresses

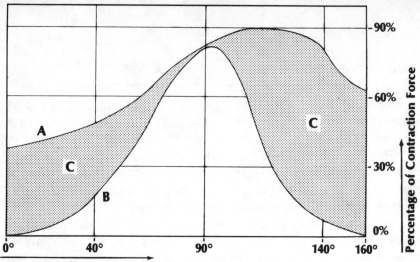

Degree of Elbow Flexion

THE BARBELL CURL VS. THE NAUTILUS CURL

The above graph compares two factors: (A) the length-tension curve of the biceps muscles and (B) the effective, or actual, resistance of a barbell curl. The shaded area (C) represents the difference between those two curves.

(A) Research shows that as the biceps contract they get stronger. The contraction force is only 35 percent as the arms start bending and increases to 90 percent as they near full flexion. At full flexion the force decreases to 65 percent. Even though the input of force reaches 100 percent, the output of usable contraction force is always smaller. Approximately 10 percent of the contraction force is wasted as a result of muscular friction and leverage factors. The ideal strength curve of the biceps muscles, therefore, should perfectly match the length-tension curve of the top line. The biceps muscles should be subjected to a resistance that is heavier at the contracted position than at the stretched position.

(B) At the start of a barbell curl (0 degrees of elbow flexion) there is no resistance, and there is no resistance at the end (140 degrees). The resistance is only correct at midflexion (90 degrees); it is too low at all other places. Thus, the barbell curl provides a bell-shaped resistance curve for the biceps muscles, which is drastically different from the ascending line of the ideal strength curve.

(C) The shaded area is the difference between the length-tension curve of the biceps muscles and the effective resistance of the barbell curl. In other words, the shaded area is the difference between ideal resistance and barbell resistance for the biceps muscles.

With the Nautilus biceps machines, the available resistance exactly follows the ideal strength curve of the biceps muscles. The resistance is never too light or too heavy. It is correct in every position. The shaded area also illustrates the amount of additional benefit for the biceps that is obtained from performing a Nautilus curl as opposed to a barbell curl.

and decreases slightly near the end. The actual rate of increase varies, depending on a number of factors, such as the muscles involved, the range of movement utilized, and the exercise performed. In all cases the resistance is exactly what it should be in every position. When an exercise is performed on a Nautilus machine, and when the set is carried to a point of momentary failure, almost 100% of the fibers contained in the muscles being worked are involved. Nautilus works almost 100% of the fibers in a muscle that are available for involvement, compared to less than 8% worked by most standard barbell exercises. Incidentally, as few as 2 or 3% of the muscle fibers are worked by a few barbell exercises.

4. Balanced resistance occurs in only one position in most barbell exercises. For example, in a curl the resistance is balanced correctly only in the sticking point that is encountered halfway through the movement. If the resistance is greater than can be handled at the sticking point, it will be impossible to pass that point and still use good form. Once the sticking point has been passed, the resistance becomes too low. It was also too low before the sticking point was reached. Thus, the resistance is only 100% correct at that one point in the movement.

The Nautilus machines provide perfectly balanced resistance that is always right—never too high and never too low. There are no sticking points and no points of little or no resistance. When you fail in such an exercise, you could fail at any point, instead of always failing at or before the sticking point, as in barbell exercises. If you are a new trainee, the resistance curve of a Nautilus machine may not feel smooth to you. You will feel no real sticking points, but the resistance probably will feel heavier toward the end of a repetition than at the start. This is to be expected, because the resistance curve is balanced to match exactly the strength curve of an individual with balanced, perfectly proportionate development. Since a man who trains with barbells has trained only part of his muscular structures (the weakest part, at that), it is inevitable that he will not be as strong as he can be.

Eventually, after you have used a Nautilus machine for a reasonable period of time, the movements will begin to feel smooth, and the opposing resistance will feel the same in all positions. Actually, that resistance will be changing constantly, even doubling, as the movement progresses from full stretch to full contracion.

5. Total muscular involvement cannot be provided by barbells for reasons that should now be obvious. Barbell exercises involve only a small portion of the total number of available muscle fibers. Nautilus machines involve almost all of the available fibers.

6. Rotary resistance is not provided by conventional exercise equipment. Barbells offer resistance that is reciprocal in nature, moving back and forth and usually up and down, but in almost all cases, it is confined to a single direction of movement. Your body parts, on the other hand, rotate, and it is evident that reciprocal resistance cannot provide appropriate resistance against a rotary form of movement. Nautilus equipment provides the required rotary form of resistance.

7. Direct resistance is rarely provided by barbells. In most

The Nautilus leg curl provides rotary, direct, variable, and balanced resistance to the hamstrings.

A typical Nautilus training room includes twelve or more Nautilus machines. (Photo Courtesy of Green Bay Packers)

barbell exercises the resistance is imposed against several muscular structures simultaneously. This would be an advantage if all the involved muscles were of equal strength. In many cases relatively small muscles become involved in the exercises as weak links. As a result, it is impossible to work the larger, stronger muscles as heavily as they must be worked for the best possible results.

Nautilus equipment overcomes this shortcoming by directing the resistance against the prime body part, rather than attempting to filter the resistance through a weaker related body part structure. For example, the latissimus dorsi muscles are attached to and move the upper arms. What happens to the hands and forearms is of no importance. So resistance is provided against the upper arms, at the elbows, as it must be in order to directly oppose movements powered by the latissimus muscles. When a point of failure is reached in such exercises it will be because the latissimus muscles are exhausted—not because the arms were too weak to continue.

When properly used, Nautilus equipment is valuable because it enormously reduces previous requirements in the way of overall training time and weekly training time. It produces better results. And Nautilus is the only exercise that is tailored to both the requirements and the limitations of the body itself.

nautilus training rules for bodybuilding

The bodybuilder's objective is to build maximum but proportional muscular size and strength in all the major muscle groups. Nautilus machines are designed scientifically around the functions of the major muscle groups of the body. Used properly, Nautilus will build maximum muscular size and strength. It should be emphasized, however, that the machines *must be used correctly*.

THE BASIC TWENTY-ONE

The following are 21 basic rules abstracted from Part I of this book. They should be applied during almost every training session.

1. Perform one set of 4–6 exercises for the lower body and 6–8 exercises for the upper body, and no more than 12 exercises in any workout.

2. Train no more than three times a week. Each workout

should involve the entire body, as opposed to splitting the routine into lower and upper body work on separate days.

3. Select resistance for each exercise that allows the performance of between 8 and 12 repetitions.

4. Continue each exercise until no additional repetitions are possible. When 12 or more repetitions can be performed, increase the resistance by approximately 5% at the next workout.

5. Position the body correctly on all single-joint rotary machines. The axis of the cam should be in line with the joint of the body part that is being exercised.

6. Keep the body properly aligned on each machine. Avoid twisting or shifting the torso and trunk during the last repetitions.

7. Work the largest muscles first and move quickly from one exercise to the next.

8. Concentrate on stretching by moving slowly during the first three repetitions of each exercise.

9. Accentuate the lowering portion of each repetition. Lift the resistance in two seconds and lower it in four seconds.

10. Move slower, never faster, if in doubt about the speed of movement.

11. Do everything possible to isolate and work each large muscle group to exhaustion.

12. Relax completely the body parts that are not involved in each exercise. Pay special attention to relaxing the face and hand muscles.

13. Move instantly from the primary to the secondary exercise on all double machines. As few as three seconds of rest can greatly reduce the pre-exhaustion benefits to the muscles.

14. Attempt constantly to increase the number of repetitions or the amount of weight, or both. But do not sacrifice form in an attempt to produce results.

15. Train with a partner who can reinforce proper form on each machine.

16. Keep accurate records—date, resistance, repetitions, and overall training time—of each workout.

17. Get ample rest after each training session. High-intensity exercise necessitates a recovery period of at least 48 hours. Muscles grow during rest, not during exercise.

18. Emphasize harder, briefer workouts as progress is made. Reduce the number of exercises from 12 to 10 and the times per week from three to two.

19. Set realistic bodybuilding goals that take into consideration such inherited factors as muscle belly lengths and skeletal structure.

20. Eat a balanced diet composed of several servings a day from the basic four food groups. Protein supplements and vitamin-mineral pills are not necessary.

21. Avoid anabolic steroids at all costs. They do not increase muscular size and strength. They are dangerous.

MAJOR BODY PARTS

The basic 21 rules must be combined with a knowledge of how to use Nautilus machines for the body's major muscles.

Bodybuilders are concerned with the development of the following body parts: hips, thighs, calves, back, shoulders, chest, upper arms, forearms, waist, and neck. The next ten chapters describe and illustrate the proper use of Nautilus machines, body part by body part. Most of the photographs used in these chapters are of Joe Means, who trains in a Nautilus gym in Columbia, South Carolina.

Joe Means is a former winner of the "Most Muscular" title in the Mr. America contest.

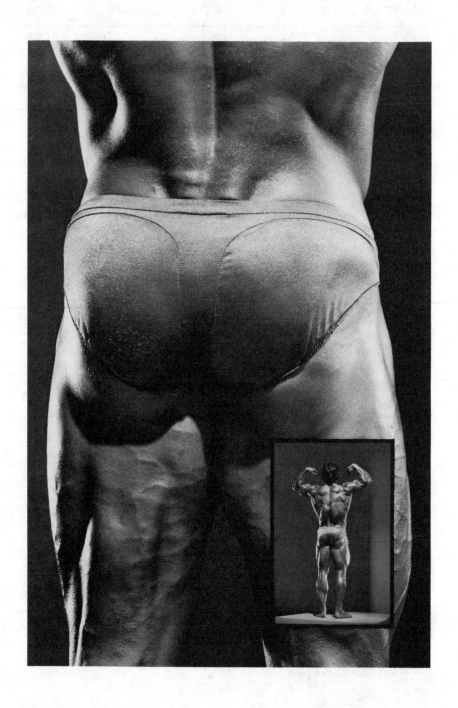

27

hips

What is the largest, strongest muscle of the entire body? It is not the quadriceps or hamstrings of the thighs; nor is it the latissimus dorsi of the upper back. And contrary to what many bodybuilders' workouts would indicate, it is not the biceps of the upper arms or the pectoralis majors of the chest. The largest, strongest muscle of the entire body is the gluteus maximus of the buttocks. This thick, powerful muscle is neglected frequently by bodybuilders out of fear that full development will somehow destroy the symmetry of the lower body. This fear is baseless. Thick, rounded buttocks add dramatic contour to the lower back, hips, and back thighs. Powerful buttock muscles are the key to lower body strength.

Bodybuilders should emphasize, rather than neglect, the gluteus maximus as well as other hip muscles.

ANATOMY OF THE HIPS

Buttocks

Starting in the middle of the hips and working toward the back, a large flat bone formation constitutes the pelvic girdle. Connected to the pelvic girdle are 22 muscles. The most important muscle of this group from the standpoint of buttock strength, shape, and size is the gluteal group, of which the *gluteus maximus* is the largest. The major function of this muscle is the extension of the hip, but only under certain conditions. In easy walking, the muscle remains relaxed until the individual tries to walk very fast, jump, walk upstairs, run, or push something. The general rule seems to be that the gluteus maximus is not called into action in the movement of the upper leg until the hip is flexed more than 45 degrees.

Full squats with a barbell have traditionally been used to develop the gluteus maximus muscles. The problem with squats is that the trainee's lower back tires before his buttocks are fatigued. Thus, the stronger muscles cannot be worked completely.

The Nautilus hip and back machine, developed in 1971, effectively solves this problem. Rather than place the resistance on the shoulders, or on the feet (as in a leg press), the resistance is placed on the back thighs, where it should be, since the buttocks extend the hip.

Outer Hips

Movement of one leg away from the other toward the side is called abduction. Hip abduction is made possible primarily by the *gluteus medius* muscles. The gluteus medius is a short, thick muscle situated at the side of the hipbone. Developed fully, it gives a rounded contour to the outer hip.

Conventional exercises for the outer hips have been limited to lifting your leg to the side while wearing a weighted boot.

The Nautilus hip abduction machine was designed and produced in 1980. It provides rotary, direct resistance for the gluteus medius muscle, which totally eliminates the need to perform weighted boot exercises.

Front Hips

The primary muscles of the front hip area are the iliacus and psoas major. The iliacus is a flat, triangular muscle that has its origin in the inner area of the pelvis and is inserted into the thigh bone. The psoas major is a long muscle that is attached to the lower portion of the spinal column. It lies beside the iliacus and also is inserted in the thigh bone. Both the iliacus and psoas have a common tendon of insertion, and, as a result, they frequently are referred to jointly as the iliopsoas.

The function of the iliopsoas is to flex the hip, or bring the knees and thighs to the chest. Bodybuilders often work the muscles unknowingly when they perform leg raises and sit-ups for the abdominals. The abdominals are exercised only mildly during leg raises and sit-ups. Most of the work is performed by the iliopsoas muscles.

Direct exercise for the iliopsoas muscles is provided by the Nautilus hip flexion machine, one of the newest Nautilus machines. Proportional development of these muscles provides a natural tie-in with the lower abdominals and upper thighs.

The Nautilus hip machines: hip and back, hip abduction, and hip flexion.

HIP AND BACK MACHINE

1. Enter machine from front by separating movement arms.
2. Lie on back with both legs over roller pads.
3. Align hip joint with axes of cams.
4. Fasten seat belt and grasp handles lightly. Seat belt should be snug, but not too tight, as back must be arched at completion of movement.

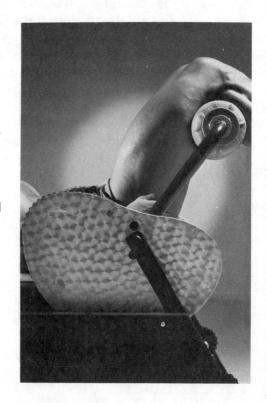

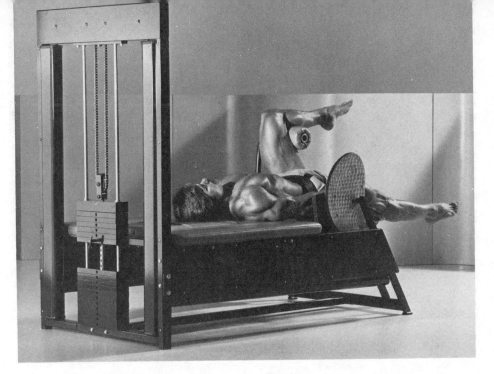

5. Extend both legs and at the same time push back with arms. With a heavy weight, extend one leg and then the other leg.
6. Keep one leg at full extension, allow other leg to bend, and come back as far as possible.
7. Stretch.

8. Push out until it joins other leg at extension.
9. Pause, arch lower back, and contract buttocks. In contracted position, keep legs straight, knees together, and toes pointed.
10. Repeat with other leg.

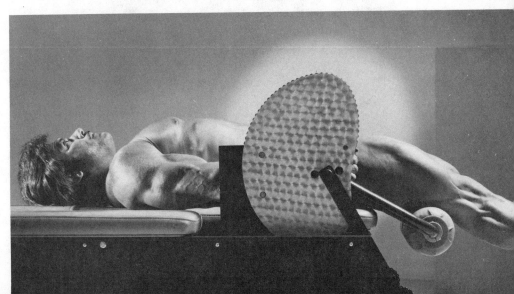

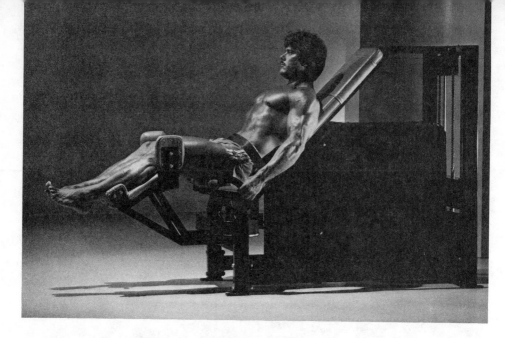

HIP ABDUCTION MACHINE

1. Sit in machine and place legs on movement arms.
2. Fasten seat belt.
3. Keep head and shoulders against seat back.

4. Spread knees and thighs to widest possible position.
5. Pause.
6. Return to knees-together position and repeat.

HIP FLEXION MACHINE

1. Sit in machine.
2. Fasten seat belt across thighs.
3. Grasp handles near your head.
4. Keep torso and head on seat back.

5. Flex hips by bringing knees to chest.
6. Pause.
7. Lower slowly to starting position and repeat.

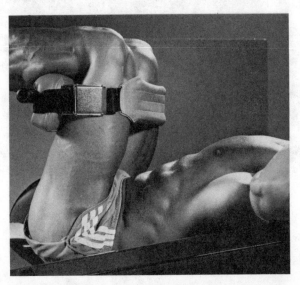

28

thighs

Well-developed thighs are the cornerstone to successful bodybuilding. The muscles of the thighs, however, must be balanced for proper symmetry. To exercise these muscles correctly, a bodybuilder must have a basic understanding of their anatomical composition.

ANATOMY OF THE THIGHS

Front Thighs

The most important muscles of the front thighs are the quadriceps. The quadriceps are composed of four muscles: vastus lateralis, vastus intermedius, vastus medialis, and rectus femoris. The vastus lateralis is located on the outer side of the thigh, and the vastus medialis is on the medial (inner) side above the kneecap. In between these muscles is the vastus intermedius. Lying on top of the vastus intermedius is the rectus femoris.

The lower tendons of all of the quadriceps muscles cross the knee joint. Full contraction of the quadriceps causes the

The front thigh muscles, or quadriceps, are clearly detailed in this pose by Joe Means.

knee to extend and the leg to straighten. Thus, leg extension movements performed with weighted boots, or on crude machines, were used by bodybuilders for years. With a standard leg extension machine, however, the range of movement around the knee joint was limited to 90 degrees, even though the possible range is at least 135 degrees.

The Nautilus leg extension machine supplies more than 135 degrees of rotary, balanced resistance for the quadriceps. Proper exercise on it stimulates the quadriceps to grow better than any other single exercise.

For best results, the leg extension, which pre-exhausts the quadriceps, should be followed immediately by the leg press. Both of these exercises can be executed on the Nautilus compound leg machine.

When properly used, the leg machine is the hardest of all Nautilus machines. To watch Mike Mentzer or Casey Viator perform both exercises back to back with the entire weight stack is an awesome sight.

Back Thighs

On the opposite side of the thighs from the quadriceps lie the hamstrings. The hamstrings include the semitendinosus,

The hamstrings are often neglected by bodybuilders. When fully developed, the hamstrings can add dramatic appeal to a posing routine.

semimembranosus, and biceps femoris muscles. The lower tendons of the three hamstring muscles cross the knee joint on the back side. When these muscles contract they bend the knee.

Before the Nautilus leg curl machine was developed, bodybuilders were forced to exercise their hamstrings by using weighted boots and crude tabletop machines. These tools were inadequate. The range of movement of the hamstrings around the knee joint exceeds 120 degrees. Only Nautilus provides full-range resistance for these important muscles.

Inner Thighs

Five muscles compose the medial or inner thigh. Of these muscles, the adductor magnus is the largest. The adductor magnus has its origin on the pubis bone and is inserted along the entire length of the thigh bone. Contraction of the adductor magnus and other inner thigh muscles brings the thighs from a spread-legged to a knees-together position. This movement is called hip adduction.

No combination of barbells and weighted boots can deliver really effective exercise for the inner thighs. The Nautilus hip adduction machine was introduced in January of 1980. It made efficient and convenient exercise for the inner thigh muscles a reality.

The Nautilus thigh machines: compound leg (leg extension and leg press), leg curl, and hip adduction.

COMPOUND LEG MACHINE

Leg Extension

1. Sit in machine.
2. Place feet behind roller pads, with knees snug against seat.
3. Adjust seat back to comfortable position.
4. Fasten seat belt.
5. Keep head and shoulders against seat back.
6. Grasp handles lightly.

7. Straighten both legs smoothly.
8. Pause.
9. Lower resistance slowly and repeat.
10. Move quickly to leg press after final repetition.

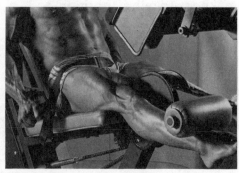

Leg Press

1. Sit erect and pull seat back forward.
2. Flip down foot pads.
3. Place both feet on pads with toes pointed slightly inward.
4. Straighten both legs in a controlled manner.
5. Avoid tightly gripping handles and do not grit teeth or tense neck or face muscles.
6. Return to stretched position and repeat.

LEG CURL MACHINE

1. Lie face down on machine.
2. Place feet under roller pads with knees just over edge of bench. Feet should be flexed toward knees.
3. Grasp handles to keep body from moving.

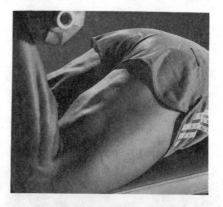

4. Curl legs and try to touch heels to buttocks.
5. Lift buttocks to increase range of movement.
6. Pause at point of full muscular contraction.

7. Lower resistance slowly and repeat.

HIP ADDUCTION MACHINE

1. Adjust lever on right side of machine for range of movement.
2. Sit in machine and place knees and ankles on movement arms in a spread-legged position. The inner thighs and knees should be firmly against the resistance pads.
3. Fasten seat belt.
4. Keep head and shoulders against seat back.

5. Pull knees and thighs smoothly together. To better isolate the adductor muscles, keep the feet pointed inward and pull with the thighs, not the lower legs.
6. Pause in knees-together position.
7. Return slowly to stretched position and repeat.

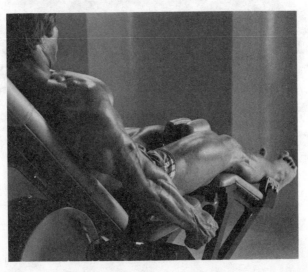

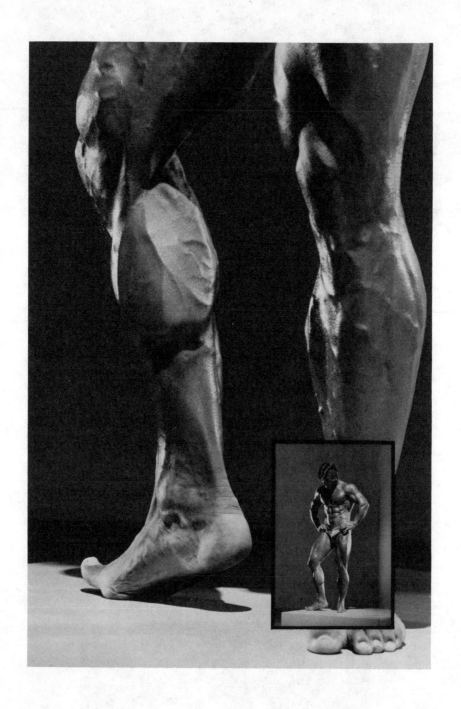

29

calves

According to bodybuilders, the calves are the most diffi- cult muscle group to develop. For several years after Arthur Jones marketed the first Nautilus machines, many body- builders desperately tried to get Jones to design a calf machine. Shaking his head and smiling to himself, he always refused.

Jones refused to build a calf machine simply because the need was not justified. "All that is required," says Jones, "is a block of wood to stand on, a heavy dumbbell for one hand, and something to hold on to for the other hand, and you're in business. Why do you need a complicated calf machine that cannot do the job any better?"

The reason the one-legged calf raise with a dumbbell is an almost perfect exercise goes back to an understanding of the physics of human movement. First, the resistance in a standing calf raise is applied directly to the prime body part, the foot. Second, the arc of the movement from the stretched position to the contracted position is such that the resistance increases as the heel rises. Third, the geometry of the involved joint and muscular attachments allows the strength curve of the calf muscles to progress throughout the movement. The one-legged calf raise therefore provides full-range direct resistance and even automatically varying resistance for the lower leg muscles.

Contrary to what many bodybuilders believe, the calves are among the easiest muscles to develop. For efficient results, however, the calf raise must be performed in the hardest possible manner.

ANATOMY OF THE CALVES

Back Calves

Eight muscles are located on the back calf. When these muscles contract, the foot extends; if you are standing, your heel is lifted from the floor.

The most important muscles in foot extension are the gastrocnemius and soleus. The gastrocnemius is the large U-shaped muscle at the back of the lower leg; when fully developed, it becomes a focal point for the entire physique, especially when viewed from the rear. Underneath the gastrocnemius lies the soleus. The soleus extends the foot primarily when the knee is flexed to 90 degrees or more.

For bodybuilding purposes it is important to work the gastrocnemius with the knee straight or locked. A four-part movement should be performed: (1) Raise the heel as high as possible. (2) Attempt to go higher by standing on the big toe. (3) Lower the heel slowly to the stretched position. (4) Try to go lower by curling and spreading the toes. This four-part movement may be performed on a four-inch step with dumbbells, conventional calf machines, or the Nautilus multi-exercise machine.

The soleus muscles are worked most efficiently in a seated position with the knees bent. Resistance is placed on top of the knees, and the heels are raised and lowered slowly.

Mike Mentzer performs a one-legged calf raise on the Nautilus multi-exercise machine. (Photo by Ellington Darden)

Front Calves

The front of the lower leg is made up of four muscles, the largest of which is the tibialis anterior. Their primary function is to flex the foot.

Foot flexions should be performed with weighted boots or by sitting forward on the Nautilus leg curl machine.

The Nautilus calf machines: leg curl (foot flexion) and multi-exercise (calf raise and seated calf raise).

MULTI-EXERCISE MACHINE

Calf Raise

1. Adjust belt comfortably around hips.
2. Place balls of feet on first step and hands on front of carriage.
3. Lock knees and keep locked throughout movement.
4. Elevate heels as high as possible and try to stand on big toes.
5. Pause.
6. Slowly lower heels.
7. Stretch at bottom by lifting and spreading toes.
8. Repeat.

Seated Calf Raise

1. Place chair in front of machine.
2. Attach small bar to movement arm.
3. Grasp handles and be seated.
4. Place handles on knees and balls of feet on first step. Front of seat may be raised with additional pads.
5. Elevate heels as high as possible.
6. Pause.

7. Slowly lower heels.
8. Stretch at bottom by lifting and spreading toes.
9. Repeat.

FOOT FLEXION ON LEG CURL MACHINE

1. Sit forward on leg curl machine.
2. Place the toes under the roller pads and lock knees. Thighs may be elevated by putting pads under knees.

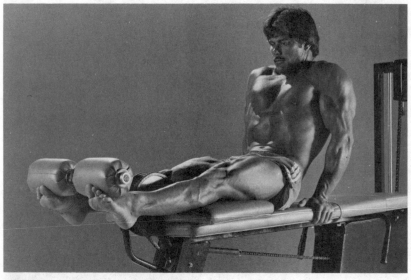

3. Flex and extend the feet against the roller pads.
4. Repeat until exhausted.

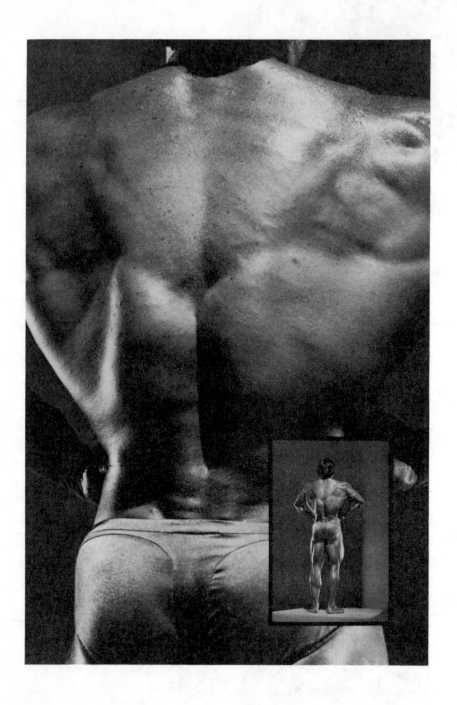

30

back

In 1970, Arthur Jones published an article entitled, "The Upper Body Squat," in which he described an exercise that would eventually revolutionize back training. "The upper body squat now exists," Jones wrote, "and it will do for the upper body just what squats have long done for the lower body."

Jones's upper body squat represented the first successful method of providing direct resistance for the largest muscles of the upper body—the latissimus dorsi. "In six weeks," wrote Jones, "we built one subject's lats to a point that normally would have required at least two full years of training."

Strong, shapely latissimus dorsi muscles give the much admired *V* shape to the physique. Two other large muscle groups, the trapezius and erector spinae, add impressive detail to the middle of the back. All the muscles of the back require direct resistance for the most efficient bodybuilding results.

The perfectly defined back of Casey Viator. Note particularly the depth and delineation among the trapezius, latissimus, and erector spinae. (Photo by John Balik)

ANATOMY OF THE BACK

The foremost muscle of the back is the latissimus dorsi. This muscle joins the lower part of the spine and sweeps up to the armpit, where it is inserted into the upper arm bone. When the latissimus dorsi muscles contract they pull the upper arms from an overhead position down and around the shoulder axes. This rotational movement can take place with the upper arms in front of the body or at the sides of the body.

Several smaller back muscles assist the latissimus in moving the upper arms. The most important of these muscles is the teres major.

The other large back muscle, the trapezius, is important in maintaining good posture. The trapezius is a flat, triangular muscle that extends from the base of the skull across the width of the shoulders and comes to a tapering point halfway down the spinal column. The most important of its functions is to elevate or shrug the shoulders. Strong trapezius muscles help support the head, shoulders, and spine.

In addition to the impressive latissimus and trapezius muscles, another area of the back is of vital importance: the lower back. This segment of the back is the foundation of

Notice the fullness of Joe Means's latissimus dorsi muscles and the thickness in his lower back area.

the body. With inadequate lower back strength, a bodybuilder cannot handle heavy movements with his upper or lower body muscles.

The primary lower back muscles are the erector spinae group. The erector spinae are composed of a large number of small paired muscles that lie on both sides of the spinal column. Extension of the spine is their major function.

Exercises for the back must take into consideration the rotational movements of the upper arms, shrugging of the shoulders, and extension of the spine.

All conventional barbell and dumbbell exercises for the back lack direct resistance for these muscles. In consequence, the smaller, weaker muscles of the arms always tire before the larger, stronger muscles of the back can be worked adequately. Chinning and pulldown movements, pullovers on a bench, shoulder shrugs with a barbell or dumbbells, and deadlifts with a barbell, are limited by the strength of the hands and arms. With a barbell it is impossible to work properly the strongest muscles of the back.

With Nautilus machines the smaller arm muscles can be bypassed and the larger back muscles worked directly. The pullover machine and behind neck machine both provide

The Nautilus back machines: behind neck/torso arm, multi-exercise (stiff-legged deadlift), pullover/torso arm, and neck and shoulder.

direct, rotary resistance for the latissimus dorsi muscles. Performing the shoulder shrug on the neck and shoulder machine effectively removes the necessity to grip in working the trapezius muscles. The hip and back machine allows the erector spinae muscles to be alternately stretched and contracted throughout a full range of movement. Furthermore, pulldowns on the torso arm machine, performed immediately after the pullover or behind neck machines, allow the bodybuilder to benefit from the pre-exhaustion technique.

PULLOVER/TORSO ARM MACHINE

Pullover

1. Adjust seat so shoulder joints are in line with axes of cams.
2. Assume erect position and fasten seat belt tightly.
3. Leg press foot pedal until elbow pads are about chin level.
4. Place elbows on pads. Hands should be open and resting on curved portion of bar.
5. Remove legs from pedal and slowly rotate elbows as far back as possible.
6. Stretch.

7. Rotate elbows downward until bar touches your midsection.
8. Pause.
9. Return slowly to stretched position and repeat. After final repetition, immediately do pulldown.

Torso Arm Pulldown

1. Lower seat to bottom for maximum stretch.
2. Grasp overhead bar with palms-up grip.

3. Keep head and shoulders against seat back.
4. Pull bar to chest.
5. Pause.
6. Return slowly to stretched position and repeat.

BEHIND NECK/TORSO ARM MACHINE

Behind Neck

1. Adjust seat so shoulder joints are in line with axes of cams.
2. Fasten seat belt.
3. Place back of upper arms, triceps area, between padded movement arms.
4. Cross forearms behind neck.

5. Move both arms downward until roller pads touch torso. Be careful not to bring arms or hands to front of body.
6. Pause.
7. Return slowly to crossed-arm position behind neck and repeat. After final repetition immediately do behind neck pulldown.

Behind Neck Pulldown

1. Lean forward and grasp overhead bar with parallel grip.

2. Pull bar behind neck, keeping elbows back.
3. Pause.
4. Return slowly to starting position and repeat.

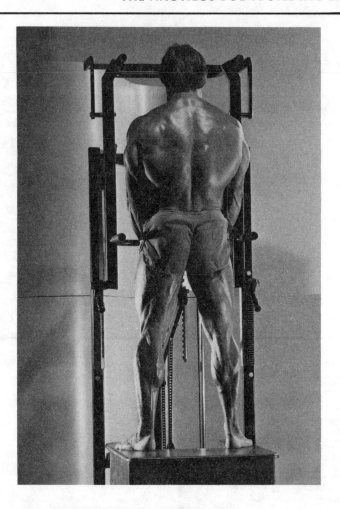

MULTI-EXERCISE MACHINE

Stiff-Legged Deadlift

1. Move a twenty-inch raised platform into position on the multi-exercise machine.
2. Attach the small handle to machine's movement arm.
3. Place feet on either side of platform.
4. Grasp handle with an under-and-over grip.
5. Lift movement arm to a standing position.

6. Keep knees locked and lower resistance to the stretched position.
7. Return to standing position and repeat.

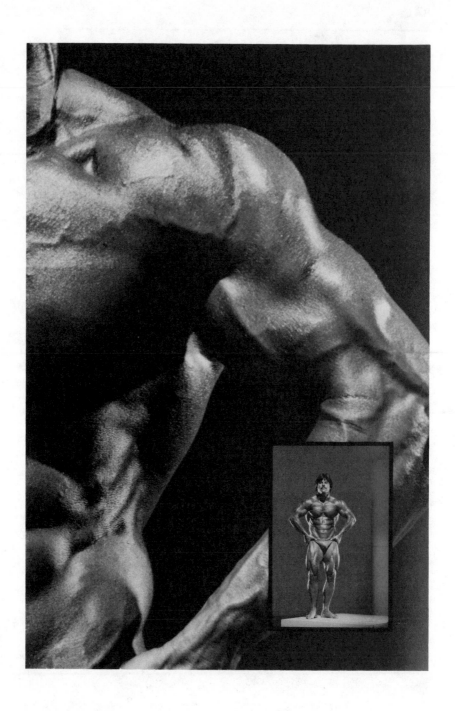

31

shoulders

In October 1978, several doctors and sports medicine people were sitting around a table at the Nautilus headquarters with Steve Reeves. Reeves, the first bodybuilder to capture public imagination, was the star of numerous Hercules movies produced in Italy in the 1960s. He was in Lake Helen to have his injured left shoulder tested and evaluated.

"How did you hurt that shoulder, Steve?" asked one of the doctors.

"I was racing a chariot. The thing got out of control and slammed into a tree." The doctors tried not to laugh.

Steve continued, "The next morning, I got chased by a crocodile and then had to swim 50 yards under water while oil burned on the surface. With every stroke, I could feel my shoulder tear a little more. But there was no turning back. I didn't want to do that scene again."

The doctors could smile now, but Reeves was still serious. His shoulder had hurt him periodically for 20 years. Even so, he inspired the admiration of millions with his well-developed physique.

Bodybuilders the world over have been motivated to develop their shoulders by watching Reeves in his heroic movie roles. Nothing sets a man off from his peers more than a muscular pair of shoulders. An old saying among manual laborers is that "Shoulders make the man." No bodybuilder ever had shoulders that were too wide.

ANATOMY OF THE SHOULDERS

Movements of the shoulder joint are produced by 11 muscles. The most important of these in size and shape is the deltoid. The deltoid, a triangular muscle, is draped over the shoulder with one angle pointing down the arm and the other two bent around the shoulder to the front and back.

The deltoid muscle is a single mass, but it is divided into three sections: anterior, middle, and posterior. Each is involved in moving the upper arm. The anterior deltoids lift the arms forward. The middle deltoids lift them sideways. The posterior deltoids lift them backward.

The deltoid muscles are divided into three sections that are clearly visible in this photograph.

Because of the varied functions of the deltoids, specific exercises should be used to develop all three sections. This assures symmetrical development and protects the shoulder joint from injury.

Conventional exercises for the deltoids are performed with dumbbells and barbells. Dumbbell exercises consist of the front raise, lateral raise, and bent-over raise, all performed with the arms straight. Basic barbell exercises include the upright row and various forms of the press.

The limitation that reduces the efficiency of all barbell and dumbbell exercises for the shoulders is the lack of rotary and direct resistance. Thus, your arms fail before you can exhaust your deltoids. To avoid this limitation, you must attach the resistance to your upper arms or elbows, rather than in your hands.

Placing the resistance against the upper arms is exactly what Arthur Jones did in designing the Nautilus double shoulder and rowing torso machines.

The Nautilus shoulder machines: double shoulder and rowing torso.

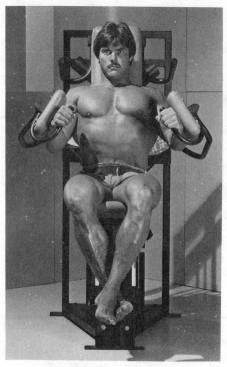

4. Lead with elbows and raise both arms until parallel with floor. Keep knuckles against pads and elbows high at all times.
5. Pause.
6. Lower resistance slowly and repeat. After final repetition, immediately do overhead press.

DOUBLE SHOULDER MACHINE

Lateral Raise

1. Adjust seat so shoulder joints with arms raised are in line with axes of cams.
2. Position thighs on seat, cross ankles, and fasten seat belt.
3. Grasp handles lightly.

Overhead Press

1. Raise seat quickly for greater range of movement.
2. Grasp handles above shoulders.

3. Press handles overhead while being careful not to arch back.
4. Lower resistance slowly, keeping elbows wide, and repeat.

ROWING TORSO MACHINE

1. Sit with back toward weight stack.
2. Place arms between pads and cross arms.

3. Bend arms in rowing fashion as far back as possible. Keep arms parallel to floor.
4. Pause.
5. Return slowly to starting position and repeat.

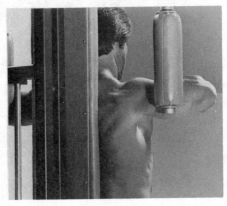

32

chest

"You just don't see that thick, high chest development anymore," declared Arthur Jones. "I remember watching George Eifferman and Clancy Ross train in 1949. They regularly used 150-pound dumbbells in performing inclined flies, and their chest developments certainly didn't suffer from it. As soon as my chest machine gets designed and built I'll guarantee that thick, high pectorals will be back in vogue."

After hearing these comments, Rocky Hutchins, a bodybuilder training at the Nautilus headquarters in Lake Helen, Florida, set his sights on attaining a George Eifferman type of chest. Rocky was a dedicated trainee. He had plenty of time to think about those thick, high pectorals. Three times a week he drove more than 300 miles round-trip from Vero Beach, and much of his driving time was spent visualizing his future chest development.

What Rocky lacked in physical potential he made up for with desire. But desire always falls short in a physique contest, and potential walks away with the trophies.

Rocky rarely let a poor showing discourage him. Regardless of the outcome of the contest, he appeared at Lake Helen every Monday, Wednesday, and Friday. Every time he trained, he asked the same question, "Has Arthur finished designing his new chest machine?"

After a physique contest in Tallahassee in which he failed to place, several of our staff noticed that Rocky was finally getting discouraged. They had an idea. The latest European bodybuilding magazine had just arrived. Its cover showed a bodybuilder from the waist up, his hands behind his head. "What if we doctored this European cover up a little?" said one of the staff. "What if we gave this bodybuilder thick, high pecs? It would sure impress Rocky, wouldn't it?"

"I've got a better idea," said another. "We have some photos around of a pair of heavyset female buttocks that we were planning on using in a hip-slimming article. We can cut out the chest area and place the buttocks behind the cover, where they'll project through. Then we'll make a print of the entire picture, buttocks and all!"

"A great idea," the staff agreed. "It might even keep Rocky interested until Arthur completes the chest machine."

The new cover was prepared. The fellows in on the joke were amazed at how real it looked. The European bodybuilder now had the thickest pectoral muscles in history.

"It makes Ross and Eifferman look like flat-chested girls," somebody said.

The big moment arrived. Rocky drove up as usual in the late afternoon.

"Hey Rocky!" said one of the fellows. "You know the old-time chest development that Arthur talks about being a thing of the past?"

"What about it?"

"Well, we've finally got the new chest machine built and

we've been secretly testing it in Europe. Take a look at this photo of one of the trainees."

"Damnation," Rocky replied as he stared at the picture. "Those are the thickest pecs I've ever seen. Book me on the next flight to Europe."

Rocky eventually figured out the joke. In the meantime Arthur designed and built the Nautilus double chest machine. And Rocky, though he never placed high in a physique contest, finally developed a chest he could be proud of.

ANATOMY OF THE CHEST

Among anatomists, the term *thorax* is used to signify the chest, and *thoracic* means anything pertaining to it. Thus the thoracic vertebrae are those vertebrae that are attached to the 12 pairs of ribs. The chest or thorax is that part of the body above the abdomen and below the head, neck, and arms. The walls of the thorax consist of ribs and breastbone and the vertebrae. These walls contain many important structures.

The bony framework of the chest is called the *rib cage*. At the rear of this cage is the spinal column, to which are attached the 12 pairs of ribs. A rib is a thin, curved strip of bone. In front the upper 10 pairs of ribs are attached to cartilages, which are fastened to the sternum or breastbone. The cartilages of the eleventh and twelfth pairs are free. These short lower ribs are called floating ribs. The general purpose of the rib cage is to protect the vital organs, primarily the heart, lungs, and liver.

The bottom of the chest cavity is formed by the large umbrella-shaped muscle of respiration known as the *diaphragm*. The diaphragm separates the chest cavity from the abdomen. Passing through the diaphragm are the esophagus and numerous arteries and nerves that connect the chest and abdominal cavities.

The massive chest development of Arnold Schwarzenegger. (Photo by Inge Cook)

Besides the diaphragm, at least six other muscles are involved in breathing, so considerable muscular contraction is necessary for even the smallest amount of inspiration. At rest, no muscular contraction is necessary for expiration. The muscles relax, and the weight of the thorax depresses the ribs, expelling some of the contents of the lungs. Under exercise conditions, however, when you are breathing deeply or rapidly, muscles are required to assist in the expiration process.

Although numerous muscles surround the chest area, the pectoralis major is the most important. It is a large fan-shaped muscle lying across the front of the chest. One edge of this muscle is attached to the sternum and the other to the front of the upper arm bone. When the pectoral muscles

The Nautilus chest machines: double chest and pullover.

contract, they pull the upper arms down and across the body.

Until the Nautilus double chest machine was designed and built in 1973, no exercise had been designed to work the pectoral muscles without involving the weaker muscles of the upper arms. Standard exercises for the chest, such as barbell bench presses and dumbbell flies, depended on the strength of the triceps. The triceps were much smaller and weaker than the pectoralis major muscles, so they became fatigued before the pectorals could be worked fully.

By placing the resistance on the elbows rather than the hands, the Nautilus double chest machine bypassed the weaker muscles of the arms. Thus, at long last, the pectoral muscles could be worked directly.

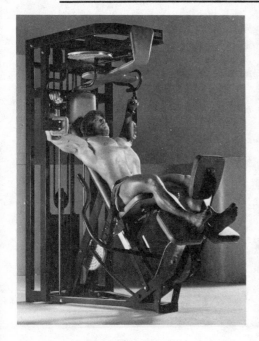

DOUBLE CHEST MACHINE

Arm Cross

1. Adjust seat until shoulders, when elbows are together, are directly under axes of overhead cams.
2. Fasten seat belt.
3. Place forearms behind and firmly against movement arm pads.
4. Grasp handles lightly with thumbs around handles, and keep head against seat back.
5. Push with forearms and try to touch elbows together in front of chest.
6. Pause.
7. Lower resistance slowly and repeat. After final repetition, immediately do decline press.

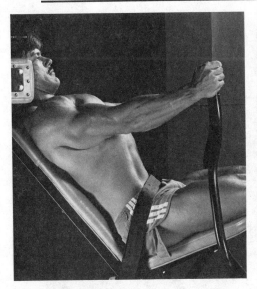

Decline Press

1. Use foot pedal to raise handles into starting position.
2. Grasp handles with parallel grip.
3. Keep head back and torso erect.
4. Press bars forward in controlled fashion.
5. Lower resistance slowly, keeping elbows wide.
6. Stretch in bottom position and repeat pressing movement.

upper arms

"BREAK THE 22-INCH BARRIER WITH MY SUPER ARM PROGRAM" reads a headline from a recent muscle magazine. "BUILD 21-INCH, HERCULEAN ARMS MY WAY" exclaims another.

"The largest arm I ever measured," says Arthur Jones, "was that of Sergio Oliva in September 1971. It was 20⅛ inches cold, measured at right angles to the bone with a tissue paper–thin tape, on the first flex after arising in the morning. Sergio's arm literally dwarfed the other arms I've seen since then. To obtain such a measurement, most bodybuilders would have to shrink the tape and cut off the first two inches, pump their arm for at least 30 minutes, and then add their forearm to the total."

Regardless of how an arm is measured, there is no doubt that bulging biceps and triceps are the goal of all bodybuilders. Nothing captures the imagination of bodybuilders more than big arms.

The arms of three Mr. Olympia winners: Arnold Schwarzenegger, Franco Columbu, and Sergio Oliva. (Photos by Inge Cook).

ANATOMY OF THE UPPER ARMS

Fifteen muscles contribute to flexion and extension of the elbow. Eight muscles control flexion and seven control extension. The most important muscle of elbow flexion is the biceps. The most important muscle of elbow extension is the triceps.

Biceps

The biceps is the prominent muscle on the front side of the upper arm. It is a two-headed muscle made up of a long and a short head. The tendons at the top end cross the shoulder joint and are attached to the scapula or shoulder blade. At the other end the tendons cross the elbow and are connected to the forearm just below the joint. The biceps crosses two joints, the shoulder and the elbow.

The function of the biceps is threefold. It supinates the hand, flexes the elbow, and lifts the upper arm forward. In order for the biceps to contract fully, the hand must be supinated, the elbow must be bent, and the upper arm must be raised to ear level.

The Nautilus compound position biceps machine was built to provide work for all three functions of the biceps. No barbell exercise can come close to duplicating this movement.

Triceps

The triceps is on the back side of the upper arm, and as its name implies, it has three separate heads: lateral, medial, and long. Like the biceps, the triceps crosses both the shoulder and the elbow joint.

The major function of the triceps is to straighten the elbow. It also assists in bringing the upper arm down from an overhead position. For the triceps to be fully contracted, the upper arm must be behind the torso as the elbow straightens.

Nautilus manufactures several types of triceps machines, all of which supply full-range exercise for these important muscles.

The Nautilus arm machines: multi-triceps, compound position biceps, multi-biceps, biceps/triceps, and multi-exercise (chin, dip, triceps extension with towel).

Compound Position Biceps Machine

1. Be seated on left side of machine to work right biceps.
2. Adjust seat so elbow is in line with axis of cam.
3. Grasp handle lightly with an underhand grip.
4. Curl handle behind neck.
5. Pause.
6. Lower movement arm slowly and repeat.
7. Reverse procedure for working left biceps on right side of machine.

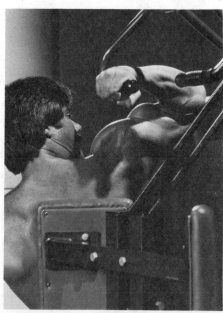

BICEPS/TRICEPS MACHINE (PLATELOADING)

Biceps Curl

1. Enter machine from left side.
2. Place elbows on pad and in line with axis of cam.
3. Grasp bar with hands together and palms up. Lean back slightly to insure stretching.

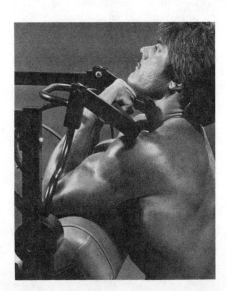

4. Curl bar smoothly until it reaches neck.
5. Pause.
6. Return slowly to stretched position and repeat.

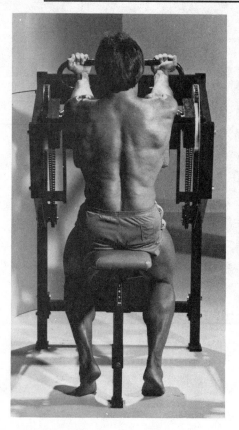

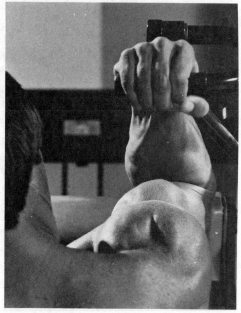

4. Curl both arms to the contracted position.
5. Pause.
6. Lower slowly to the stretched position and repeat.

MULTI-BICEPS MACHINE

1. Place elbows on pad and in line with the axes of cams.
2. Adjust seat so shoulders are slightly lower than elbows.
3. Grasp handles lightly.

This machine may be used in several other ways: two arms duo-poly, one arm normal, one arm negative-emphasized, and infimetric.

MULTI-EXERCISE MACHINE

Chin (Negative-Only with or without Weight Belt)

1. Place crossbar in forward position.
2. Adjust carriage to proper height. When standing on top step, chin should be barely over bar.
3. Grasp crossbar with palms up. Movement can also be done in a behind neck fashion.
4. Climb steps.
5. Place chin over bar, elbows by sides, and legs bent.
6. Lower body slowly (eight to ten seconds).
7. Stretch at bottom position.
8. Climb up and repeat.

BICEPS/TRICEPS MACHINE

Triceps Extension

1. Adjust seated position, with pads if necessary, until the shoulders are on same level as elbows on axis of rotation.
2. Place elbows in line with axis of cam and hands with thumbs up on pads.

3. Straighten arms smoothly.
4. Pause.
5. Return slowly to stretched position and repeat.

MULTI-TRICEPS MACHINE

1. Adjust seat so shoulders are slightly lower than elbows.
2. Place sides of hands on movement arms and elbows on pad and in line with the axes of cams.

3. Straighten arms to the contracted position.
4. Pause.
5. Lower slowly to the stretched position and repeat.

This machine may be used in several other ways: two arms alternate, two arms duo-poly, one arm normal, one arm negative-emphasized, and infimetric.

MULTI-EXERCISE MACHINE

Parallel Dip (Negative-Only with or without Weight Belt)

1. Adjust carriage to proper level. It is important to allow ample stretch in bottom position.
2. Climb steps.
3. Lock elbows and bend legs.
4. Lower body slowly by bending arms (eight to ten seconds).
5. Stretch at bottom position.
6. Climb up and repeat.

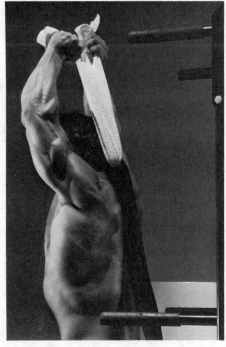

MULTI-EXERCISE MACHINE

Triceps Extension with Towel

1. Loop a lightweight towel through weight belt.
2. Grasp one end of towel in each hand. Stand and face away from machine. Arms should be bent with elbows near ears.
3. Adjust grip on towel until weight stack is separated.

4. Straighten arms in a very smooth fashion.
5. Pause.
6. Lower resistance slowly and repeat.

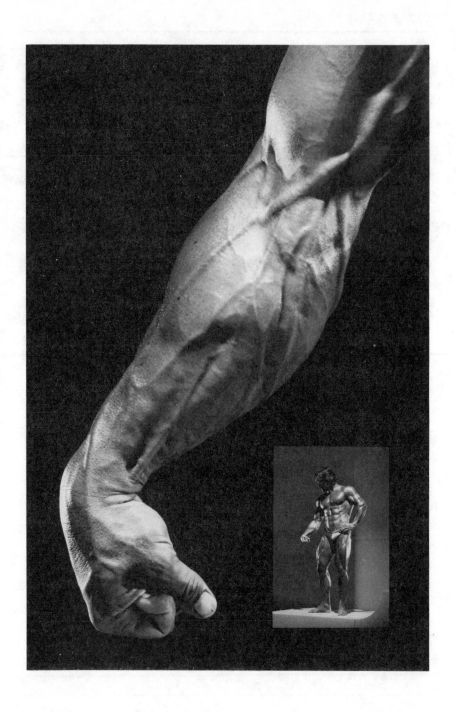

34

forearms

Many people have seen the movie about Popeye, that funny little man with the sailor hat and a tremendous affinity for spinach. For some strange reason, Popeye's creator chose to depict this epitome of male strength with large muscular forearms. Regardless of the size of his chest, shoulders, and legs, it took only one can of spinach for Popeye to pulverize his formidable opponent.

Although Popeye may have ignored some body parts in his training program, he certainly did not neglect the muscles of his forearms. Neglect of the forearms is a common mistake among bodybuilders. The forearms are one of the easiest body parts to strengthen. They are among the few muscle groups that can be worked directly, without using the weaker muscles that tire before the primary ones.

ANATOMY OF THE FOREARMS

Nineteen separate muscles make up the forearm. These muscles act on both the fingers and the wrist. The bulk of

The forearm extensor muscles.

The Nautilus multi-exercise machine can be used to perform the wrist curl and reverse wrist curl.

the musculature is concentrated in two masses just below the elbow joint. The mass on the outside of the forearm is formed by the bellies of the extensor muscles. The inside mass of the forearm comes from the bellies of the flexor muscles.

The forearms are very complex structures. Disregarding the flexion of the forearm against the upper arm, which is primarily caused by the biceps of the upper arm, the functions of the forearm include: supination of the hand, pronation of the hand, gripping, extension of the fingers, and flexion of the hand in four separate directions.

Exercise properly performed for wrist flexion and wrist extension indirectly provides adequate work for the other, smaller forearm muscles. It is not necessary to devise an exercise for each forearm function. Both wrist flexion and wrist extension can be performed on the Nautilus multi-exercise machine.

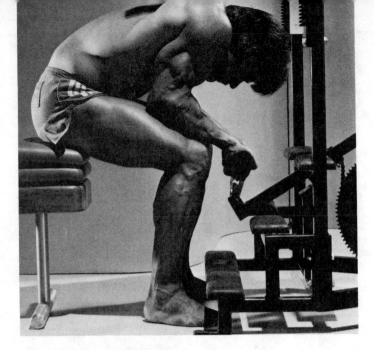

MULTI-EXERCISE MACHINE

Wrist Curl

1. Sit in front of machine, using small bench or chair, with toes under first step.
2. Attach small bar directly to movement arm.
3. Grasp handles in a palms-up fashion.
4. Place forearms firmly against thighs.
5. Lean forward to isolate forearm flexors. The angle between the biceps and forearms should be less than 90 degrees.

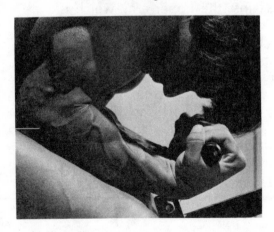

6. Curl small bar upward.
7. Pause.
8. Lower resistance slowly and repeat.

MULTI-EXERCISE MACHINE

Reverse Wrist Curl

1. Sit in front of machine, using a small bench or chair, with toes under first step.
2. Attach small bar directly to movement arm.
3. Grasp handles in a palms-down fashion.
4. Place forearms firmly against thighs.

5. Reverse curl small bar upward.
6. Pause.
7. Lower resistance slowly and repeat.

35

waist

Arthur Jones said roughly the following in his *Bulletin No. 2:* "Spot reduction of fatty tissue is an outright myth—a physical impossibility. Build the muscles of your abdominal area by training them in exactly the same way you exercise your other muscles: one set of 8 to 12 repetitions, repeated three times weekly. Get rid of any fat in that area by simply reducing your intake of calories or by increasing your expenditure of calories, but *not* by increasing the amount of abdominal exercise. In effect, you can reduce fatty tissue in the area of the waist by working your legs, arms, shoulders, or any other muscle group in your body. It is not necessary to work the midsection in order to reduce fat in the midsection. And *absolutely nothing* in the way of an artificial aid will do anything to help the situation. What matters most is your overall consumption of calories, your energy output versus your energy input."

This concept is not new. It has been proved repeatedly through scientific experimentation over the last 50 years. Yet, high-repetition exercise for the waist remains one of the strangest fallacies in bodybuilding history. Many bodybuilders do sit-ups and leg raises by the thousands under the mistaken belief that it will remove midsection fat and develop the abdominal muscles.

The abdominals are important muscles. Many a physique contest has been won or lost on their strength or weakness. A well-defined waistline makes the chest look fuller and the shoulders broader. But all bodybuilders should understand that a muscular waistline is never the result of high-repetition sit-ups or leg raises.

The condition of the waist is controlled by three factors: (1) genetics, (2) percentage of body fat, and (3) muscular development of the abdominals and obliques.

The importance of genetics in bodybuilding cannot be overemphasized. How and where an individual stores fat is basically determined prior to and just after birth. As stated previously, in Chapter 17, bodybuilders with dark skin and eyes have a greater potential for leanness and muscularity than do bodybuilders with light skin and blue eyes. The

A lean, well-defined waistline makes the shoulders look broader.

shape and symmetrical pairing of the abdominal muscles is also based on inheritance.

A bodybuilder must reduce his percentage of subcutaneous body fat if he wishes his waistline to become more defined. The chemistry of losing body fat is based on the fact that there are 3,500 calories in one pound of fat. Thus, a bodybuilder's caloric output must exceed his caloric input in order to shrink his existing fat cells. A well-balanced low-calorie diet practiced for several months is the most efficient way to lose subcutaneous fat. But where the fat is lost and to what degree, once again, is determined genetically. Fat rarely, if ever, is lost from only one spot.

Development of the midsection should be based on a general understanding of the anatomy and function of its musculature.

ANATOMY OF THE WAIST

For bodybuilding purposes, the waist is composed of front and side muscles. The most important muscle of the front waist is the rectus abdominis. The external and internal obliques compose the side waist.

Rectus Abdominis

The rectus abdominis is attached to the fifth, sixth, and seventh ribs; extends across the front of the abdominal wall; and joins the pubis bone. The function of the rectus abdominis is to shorten the distance between the lower portion of the sternum and the pelvic girdle. To illustrate: Lie flat on your back. Roll your shoulders and head up and forward. At the same time, raise your hips upward and back toward the chest. This movement is the primary action caused by the contraction of the rectus abdominis.

Sit-ups and leg raises are not abdominal exercises. They work the iliopsoas or hip flexor muscles. When the iliopsoas muscles contract they pull the upper body to a sitting position, or they pull the thighs toward the chest. The rectus

When contracted, the rectus abdominis muscles exhibit five paired formations.

abdominis is only mildly involved in a traditional sit-up or leg raise.

The difficulty of exercising the abdominal muscles was solved in 1980 by the production of the Nautilus abdominal machine. This new invention effectively isolates and works the rectus abdominis to a degree not possible with standard exercises or equipment.

External and Internal Obliques

High-repetition exercises have also been the rule in working the oblique muscles. Bodybuilders everywhere perform thousands of twisting movements with an empty bar and thousands of side bends with light dumbbells in their attempts to remove fatty deposits from their sides. Little is accomplished from such exercises.

Many bodybuilders fear that heavy exercise for the obliques will produce a bulky appearance of the waist. This is incorrect. No bodybuilder has ever developed oblique muscles that were too large. Many bodybuilders have obliques that are underdeveloped. What usually happens is that the thick layer of fat overlying the obliques is thought to be muscle. The remedy is a low-calorie diet, not high-repetition exercise.

The external oblique muscles are attached to the lower ribs and extend around the outer waist until they join the hipbone. The primary function of the external oblique is to bend the spine to the same side and to rotate the torso to the opposite side.

The internal oblique is a sheath of muscle beneath the external oblique. The fibers run at right angles to those of the outer muscle. Lateral flexion to the same side and torso rotation to the same side are the main functions of the internal oblique muscles.

Other muscles also contribute to torso rotation. Among them are several muscles of the erector spinae and deep posterior spinal groups.

The traditional way to work the torso rotation muscles was to place a light barbell across the shoulders and perform twisting movements while seated. Since the barbell was being rotated horizontally, little resistance was ever applied to the external and internal obliques. The muscles were merely being stretched.

In the summer of 1981, after years of research, Nautilus introduced the rotary torso machine. It is the first device to provide effective, full-range exercise for the external and internal obliques.

The Nautilus waist machines: rotary torso, multi-exercise (side bend), and abdominal.

ABDOMINAL MACHINE

1. Sit in machine.
2. Locate axis of rotation of machine that is parallel to separation in seat back. Lower part of sternum should be at this level.
3. Adjust seat by depressing handle under seat bottom.
4. Place ankles behind roller pads.
5. Spread knees and sit erect.
6. Grasp handles over shoulders.
7. Keep shoulders and head firmly against seat back.

8. Shorten the distance between rib cage and navel by contracting abdominals only. Do not pull with latissimus or triceps muscles.
9. Keep legs relaxed as seat bottom is elevated.
10. Pause in contracted position.
11. Return slowly to starting position and repeat.

MULTI-EXERCISE MACHINE

Side Bend

1. Attach belt or handle to movement arm.
2. Grasp handle in left hand with left shoulder facing machine.
3. Assume a standing position.
4. Place right hand on top of head.

5. Bend to left side.
6. Return to standing position and repeat.
7. Change hands and do side bend to right side.

ROTARY TORSO MACHINE

1. Face front of machine while standing. Weight stack should be in back.
2. Place seat yoke (adjustment is underneath) approximately 90 degrees to left of weight stack (new machine has a yoke on both sides so no adjustment is necessary).
3. Straddle seat and cross ankles securely. Do not allow hips and legs to move with torso.
4. Turn to left and place forearms on sides of pads. Left palm should be firmly against middle bar of movement arm.

5. Rotate torso from left to right by pushing with left palm. Do not use triceps or biceps to push or pull the movement arm. Use the torso rotators.
6. Move head with torso by focusing between parallel bars of movement arm.
7. Pause in contracted position. Rotation of torso will be less than 180 degrees.
8. Return slowly to starting position and repeat.
9. Adjust yoke to opposite side of machine and reverse procedure for right-to-left torso rotation.

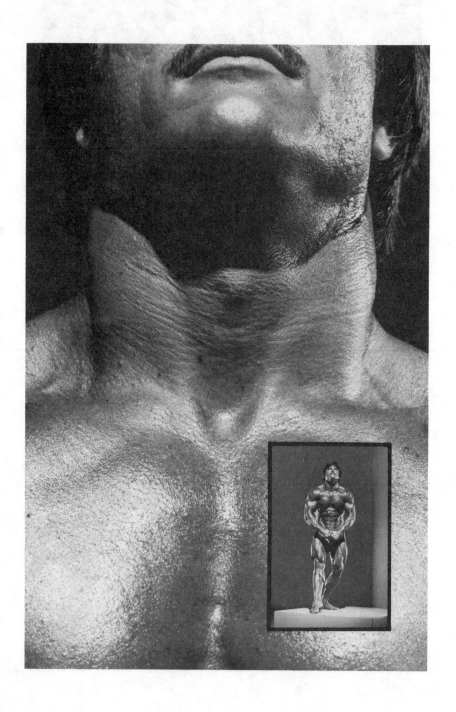

36

neck

The muscles most widely ignored by the average body-builder are those of the neck. Two facts encourage this tendency. First, some so-called experts advise against neck work. They reason that a large neck will detract from shoulder width. This makes about as much sense as never developing the lower body so that the upper body will look larger. All-over symmetry should be the goal of bodybuilding, and it comes from the pleasing development of all major muscle groups. Second, until recently there has been no practical method of directly exercising the neck. Most available exercises were clumsy, difficult, uncomfortable, and often dangerous. As a result, this important area was neglected.

Fortunately, the neck responds quickly to the right kind of exercise. In fact, the muscles of the neck are among the easiest to develop.

The trapezius muscles of the upper back, neck, and shoulders can be seen in this back pose by Joe Means.

ANATOMY OF THE NECK

When man assumed the upright position, the huge muscles of the nape of the neck gradually atrophied. Now man balances his head, weighing about 14 pounds, on seven small cervical vertebrae. The only restraints to sudden movements of the neck are the strength and integrity of the cervical vertebrae, the spinal ligaments, and the neck muscles. It is essential, therefore, to strengthen and develop this protective musculature.

At least 15 small and medium-sized muscles, the most

The Nautilus neck machines: rotary neck, 4-way neck, and neck and shoulder.

important of which is the sternocleidomastoids, make up the bulk of the neck. These muscles are capable of producing movement in seven different directions:

1. Elevating the shoulders
2. Bending the head toward the chest
3. Drawing the head backward
4. Bending the head down toward the right shoulder
5. Bending the head down toward the left shoulder
6. Twisting the head to look over the right shoulder
7. Twisting the head to look over the left shoulder

In 1975 Nautilus introduced three machines—the four-way neck, rotary neck, and neck and shoulder—that were specifically designed to provide direct exercise for the neck's seven functions. When full-range exercise is provided for these seven functions, the response of the neck muscles is immediate. The neck responds quickly to exercise because its muscles are exposed to so little hard work. Development of the neck muscles, therefore, is not a matter of years but of weeks.

4-WAY NECK MACHINE

Anterior Flexion

1. Face machine.
2. Adjust seat so that your nose is in center of pads.
3. Stabilize torso by lightly grasping handles.

4. Move head smoothly toward chest.
5. Pause.
6. Return slowly to stretched position and repeat.

Posterior Extension

1. Turn body in machine until back of head contacts center of pads.
2. Stabilize torso by lightly grasping handles.

3. Extend head as far back as possible.
4. Pause.
5. Return slowly to stretched position and repeat.

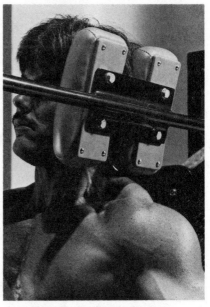

Lateral Contraction

1. Turn body in machine until left ear is in center of pads.
2. Stabilize torso by lightly grasping handles.
3. Move head toward left shoulder.
4. Pause.
5. Keep shoulders square.
6. Return slowly to stretched position and repeat.
7. Reverse procedure for right side.

ROTARY NECK MACHINE

1. Sit facing away from machine.
2. Move head between pads.
3. Adjust head pads to a snug position by pulling overhead lever from right to left.

4. Push hand levers to provide resistance in this machine. Negative-only exercise can be provided by pressure on either hand lever, which will force head to turn. This turning pressure is resisted by neck muscles.
5. Push with right-hand lever, or pull with left-hand lever, to force neck and head to rotate to the left or vice versa.

6. Alternately perform six negative-only repetitions to the right and six negative-only repetitions to the left.
7. Release head pads by pulling overhead lever from left to right.

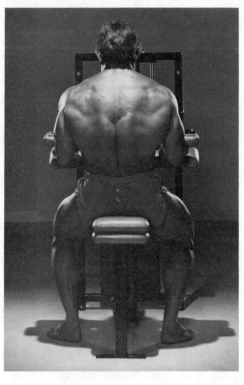

NECK AND SHOULDER MACHINE

1. Place forearms between pads while seated.
2. Keep palms open and back of hands pressed against bottom pads.
3. Straighten torso until weight stack is lifted. The seat may be raised with elevation pads.

4. Smoothly shrug shoulders as high as possible. Keep elbows by sides when shrugging. Do not lean back.
5. Pause.
6. Return slowly to stretched position and repeat.

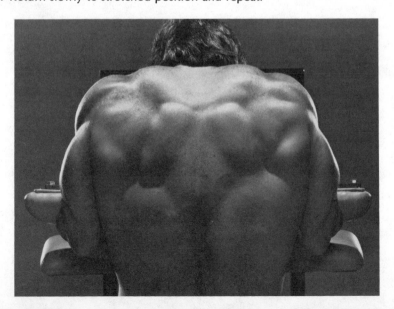

37

organizing nautilus routines

In organizing a successful bodybuilding program using Nautilus equipment, the following rules should be observed:

- Perform one set of 4–6 exercises for the lower body, and 6–8 for the upper body, and no more than 12 exercises in any workout.
- Train no more than three times a week. Each workout should involve the entire body, as opposed to splitting the routine into lower and upper body work on separate days.
- Work the largest muscles first.
- Keep accurate records—date, resistance, repetitions, and overall training time—of each workout.

These rules apply to the master listing of Nautilus exercises. The listing includes the major body parts discussed in the last 10 chapters.

MASTER LISTING OF EXERCISES

Body Part	Nautilus Machine or Exercise
Hips	Hip and Back
	Hip Abduction
	Hip Flexion
	Stiff-Legged Deadlift
Thighs	Leg Extension
	Leg Press
	Leg Curl
	Hip Adduction
Calves	Calf Raise on Multi-Exercise
	Seated Calf Raise on Multi-Exercise
	Foot Flexion on Leg Curl
Back	Pullover/Torso Arm
	Pullover
	Torso Arm Pulldown
	Behind Neck/Torso Arm
	Behind Neck
	Behind Neck Pulldown
	Neck and Shoulder
	Hip and Back
Shoulders	Double Shoulder
	Lateral Raise
	Overhead Press
	Rowing Torso
Chest	Double Chest
	Arm Cross
	Decline Press
	Pullover
Upper Arms	Compound Position Biceps Curl
	Biceps Curl (plateloading)
	Multi-Biceps Curl
	Chin on Multi-Exercise
	Triceps Extension (plateloading)
	Multi-Triceps Extension
	Triceps Extension with Towel on Multi-Exercise
	Dip on Multi-Exercise

Forearms	Wrist Curl on Multi-Exercise
	Reverse Wrist Curl on Multi-Exercise
Waist	Abdominal
	Rotary Torso
	Side Bend on Multi-Exercise
Neck	4-Way Neck
	Rotary Neck
	Neck and Shoulder

BASIC ROUTINES

Variety in training is an important consideration for most bodybuilders. There is no *single* ideal routine; there are many. The following routines provide examples of effective grouping and ordering of Nautilus exercises. If certain Nautilus machines are not available, substitutions can be made.

Note: Bodybuilders who train on Nautilus equipment in commercial fitness centers should make certain that they have the management's approval before any listed routine is tried. Under some circumstances, it is neither practical nor advisable to perform certain exercises or routines.

I	II
Basic Nautilus Workout	*Basic Nautilus Workout*
1. Hip and Back	1. Hip and Back
2. Hip Adduction	2. Hip Abduction
3. Leg Extension	3. Leg Extension
4. Leg Curl	4. Calf Raise
5. Pullover	5. Behind Neck
6. Pulldown	6. Behind Neck Pulldown
7. Lateral Raise	7. Dip
8. Overhead Press	8. Rowing Torso
9. Neck and Shoulder	9. Triceps Extension
10. Arm Cross	10. Biceps Curl
11. Decline Press	11. Abdominal
12. 4-Way Neck	12. Neck and Shoulder

III

Basic
Nautilus Workout

1. Leg Curl
2. Hip Adduction
3. Leg Press
4. Hip Flexion
5. Pullover
6. Overhead Press
7. Chin
8. Dip
9. Wrist Curl
10. Reverse Wrist Curl
11. Abdominal
12. Rotary Torso

IV

Basic
Nautilus Workout

1. Stiff-Legged Deadlift
2. Leg Extension
3. Leg Press
4. Leg Curl
5. Calf Raise
6. Lateral Raise
7. Overhead Press
8. Pullover
9. Pulldown
10. Arm Cross
11. Decline Press
12. Neck and Shoulder

V

Basic
Nautilus Workout

1. Hip Adduction
2. Hip Abduction
3. Hip and Back
4. Hip Flexion
5. Behind Neck
6. Chin
7. Decline Press
8. Rowing Torso
9. Multi-Triceps Extension
10. Multi-Biceps Curl
11. Abdominal
12. Rotary Neck

VI

Basic
Nautilus Workout

1. Leg Press
2. Leg Extension
3. Calf Raise
4. Foot Flexion
5. Leg Curl
6. Lateral Raise
7. Pullover
8. Decline Press
9. Wrist Curl
10. Reverse Wrist Curl
11. 4-Way Neck
12. Rotary Torso

Occasionally, it is a good idea for a bodybuilder to work his arms separately rather than together. (Photo by Ellington Darden)

ALTERNATE ROUTINES

After you have tried the basic routines you may decide to follow one of the Nautilus negative workouts listed below once a week. Eventually, you will want to experiment with other alternate workouts or design your own routine according to the rules given at the beginning of this chapter.

Again, it is important to realize that it may not be possible to apply certain techniques in commercial facilities. Be sure to check with the management before performing any routine described below.

Abbreviations Used in Describing the Exercises and Styles of Training

(NO)—Negative-only exercise: the positive portion of an exercise movement is performed by assistants or by the trainee's legs as a heavier-than-normal weight is slowly lowered by the trainee.

(NA)—Negative-accentuated exercise: the trainee lifts the resistance with two limbs and slowly lowers with one limb.

(NE)—Negative-emphasized exercise: a lighter-than-normal weight is used on the positive part of the movement;

additional resistance is then provided on the negative phase by an assistant pressing down on the weight stack.

VII	VIII
Negative Nautilus Workout	*Negative Nautilus Workout*
1. Leg Extension (NA)	1. Hip Abduction (NE)
2. Leg Press (NA)	2. Leg Curl (NE)
3. Leg Curl (NA)	3. Leg Press (NE)
4. Hip Adduction (NE)	4. Leg Extension (NE)
5. Pullover (NO)	5. Rowing Torso (NE)
6. Chin (NO)	6. Decline Press (NO)
7. Lateral Raise (NO)	7. Pullover (NA)
8. Overhead Press (NO)	8. Overhead Press (NA)
9. Neck and Shoulder (NE)	9. Abdominal (NO)
10. Dip (NO)	10. 4-Way Neck (NO)

According to Arthur Jones, "A properly performed set on the Nautilus compound leg machine should leave you feeling like you just climbed a tall building with your car tied to your back."

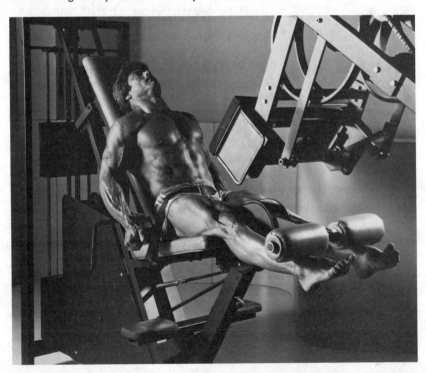

IX

Nautilus
Pre-Exhaustion Workout

1. Leg Curl
2. Hip Adduction
3. Hip and Back
4. Leg Extension
5. Leg Press
6. Pullover
7. Behind Neck
8. Behind Neck Pulldown
9. Triceps Extension
10. Dip (NO)
11. Biceps Curl
12. Chin (NO)

X

Nautilus
Pre-Exhaustion Workout

1. Leg Curl
2. Leg Extension
3. Leg Press
4. Behind Neck Pulldown
5. Behind Neck
6. Chin (NO)
7. Decline Press
8. Arm Cross
9. Dip (NO)
10. Abdominal
11. Rotary Torso
12. Pullover

In routines **IX** and **X**, rest only between exercises separated by the rules.

XI

Nautilus
Push-and-Pull Workout

1. Hip Abduction
2. Hip Adduction
3. Leg Extension
4. Leg Curl
5. Overhead Press
6. Chin
7. Decline Press
8. Behind Neck Pulldown
9. Dip
10. Pullover
11. Triceps Extension
12. Biceps Curl

XII

Nautilus
Push-and-Pull Workout

1. Hip and Back
2. Hip Flexion
3. Leg Curl
4. Leg Press
5. Chin
6. Dip
7. Behind Neck
8. Overhead Press
9. Neck and Shouder
10. Rotary Neck
11. Side Bend
12. 4-Way Neck

XIII

Nautilus
Change-of-Pace Workout

1. Overhead Press
2. Chin
3. Decline Press
4. Pullover
5. Dip
6. Rowing Torso
7. Leg Extension
8. Leg Curl
9. Triceps Extension with Towel
10. Compound Position Biceps

XIV

Nautilus
Change-of-Pace Workout

1. Leg Press (Seat back)
2. Pullover
3. Leg Press (Seat close)
4. Behind Neck
5. Calf Raise
6. Abdominal
7. Dip
8. Triceps Extension
9. Chin
10. Biceps Curl
11. Stiff-Legged Deadlift

38

questions please!

THE NAUTILUS CAM

Q. *What effect does the Nautilus cam have on the productivity of an exercise?*

A. The heart of every Nautilus machine is the exclusive Nautilus cam, the spiral-shaped pulley that automatically and instantly varies the resistance as movement occurs.

When you perform a repetition on a Nautilus machine, you become stronger or weaker, depending on the direction of movement. The Nautilus cam instantly compensates for the resulting change in strength. It automatically increases or reduces the resistance to match your changing strength.

With barbell exercises you are always limited by your strength in the weakest position. Thus, you never encounter enough resistance in the stronger positions. Nautilus provides correct resistance in every position: lower in your weaker positions, higher in your stronger positions, and maximum in your strongest position.

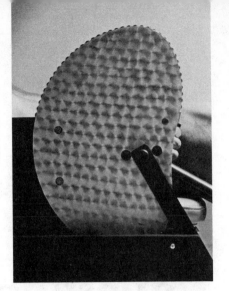

Resistance must vary throughout the movement, changing in proportion to the strength of the involved muscles in various positions. The Nautilus cam makes variable and balanced resistance possible on each Nautilus machine.

The Nautilus cam is the only practical method of automatically changing the available resistance during the actual movement. It does so by automatically changing the moment arm, and thus the torque.

Muscular contraction produces torque, or rotary force around an axis. Torque is the result of two factors: the length of the moment arm and the amount of weight you use. If you double the length of the moment arm, you double the torque, even though the weight remains constant.

In a Nautilus machine the selected weight can be as much or as little as you require, and the weight remains constant during the exercise. But the Nautilus cam varies the moment arm as movement occurs, thus increasing or reducing the effective resistance—the torque.

Barbell exercises work only part of a muscle, but Nautilus works all of a muscle. Quite simply, there is no other method of providing this important requirement for full-range exercise.

REPETITIONS FOR DEFINITION AND BULK

Q. *Is it better to concentrate on performing high repetitions for definition and low repetitions for bulk?*

A. Both of these assumptions are incorrect.

Ninety-nine percent of muscular definition has to do with

a person's overall body fat content, which is primarily a result of genetics and dietary calories. High repetitions have virtually no effect on muscular definition. If you desire greater definition, you must reduce your percentage of body fat by adhering to a balanced low-calorie diet. But even then your potential definition is limited by your genes.

Muscular bulk or size is best produced by intensive exercise that lasts at least 30 seconds, but not more than 70 seconds. If a typical repetition of an exercise takes about 6 seconds to perform, simple multiplication reveals that 8 repetitions would take 48 seconds, and 12 repetitions 72 seconds. Thus, performing an exercise for fewer than 8 repetitions is not as effective in building muscular bulk as is doing repetitions in the 8 to 12 range.

The symmetrical physique of Dan Tobol, a former Teenage Mr. America. In this picture, Tobol weighed 232 pounds at a height of 6 feet, one inch. (Photo by Ken Neely)

RELAXATION OF THE FACE

Q. *Is there a simple way to learn to relax the face during the last repetitions of an exercise?*

A. One of the basic cornerstones of bodybuilding is muscle isolation. A muscle is better isolated if you relax the uninvolved body parts, especially the face.

In most cases learning to relax the uninvolved body parts begins with the face. If your jaw is contracted, you cannot be relaxed. An excellent way to relax the jaw and face is to relax the tongue. The tongue is relaxed by slightly dropping the jaw and letting the tongue lie against the lower teeth. When the tongue is relaxed it is almost impossible to contract the facial muscles intensely.

THE EASY-CURL BAR

Q. *Why are curls with an easy-curl bar less beneficial to the biceps than curls done with a straight bar?*

A. The best way to answer this question is to discuss another one first. Why can you curl more weight on a barbell with a palms-up grip than with a palms-down grip? Because with a palms-down grip, the biceps are forced into a position at which they cannot function fully. It is important to remember that the primary function of the biceps is to supinate the hand, moving it from a palms-down to a palms-up position.

An easy-curl bar moves the hand in the direction of pronation rather than supination. It does not fully pronate

The primary function of the biceps is to supinate the hands. The easy-curl bar twists the hands in the direction of pronation, rather than supination. Thus, straight-bar curls are better for developing the biceps than curls performed with an easy-curl bar.

the hand, but it goes at least part of the way, too far to permit the biceps to function best. Thus, any exercise for the biceps, or any exercise that involves both the biceps and torso muscles, should be performed with a fully supinated palms-up grip.

BARBELL WORKOUT

Q. *Does Nautilus have a recommended bodybuilding workout with barbells for people who do not have access to Nautilus equipment?*

A. The same basic principles that are used to organize a bodybuilding routine with Nautilus machines can be applied to barbells and conventional equipment. Three times a week you should perform 4–6 exercises for the lower body and 6–8 exercises for the upper body. A workout should consist of no more than one set of 12 different exercises.

There are many effective sequences of basic barbell exercises. An example of one program is listed below:

1. Squat (barbell)
2. Stiff-legged deadlift (barbell)
3. Leg press (leg press machine)
4. One-legged calf raise (dumbbell)
5. Bent-armed pullover (barbell)
6. Standing press (barbell)
7. Bent-over rowing (barbell)
8. Decline press (barbell)
9. Shoulder shrug (barbell or dumbbells)
10. Standing triceps extension (dumbbell)
11. Standing biceps curl (barbell)
12. Side bend (dumbbell)

ANGLE TRAINING

Q. *Bodybuilding magazines frequently advocate training a muscle from different angles. What does Nautilus have to say about angle training?*

A. An example of recommended angle training is the following: Perform incline presses for the upper pectorals, bench presses for the middle pectorals, and decline presses for the lower pectorals. If that is not enough, you can vary your hand spacing. Wide-grip presses work the outer pectorals and narrow-grip presses work the inner pectorals.

Everything in the paragraph above is faulty. The function of the pectoral muscles is to move the upper arms down and across the front of the torso. You can demonstrate this by

A wide-grip bench press provides a range of movement of 69 degrees around the shoulders. Performed with a narrow grip, the same exercise provides approximately 90 degrees of movement, or a difference of 21 degrees. If in doubt about which of several exercises to perform, always choose the exercise that involves the greatest range of movement.

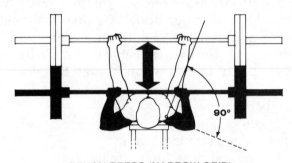

BENCH PRESS (NARROW GRIP)

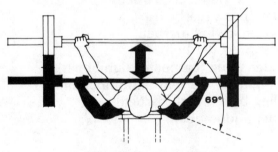

BENCH PRESS (WIDE GRIP)

The best barbell exercise for the pectoralis major muscles of the chest is the decline bench press.

standing with your arms out to your sides. Now raise the elbows to about eye level and force the elbows back and the rib cage forward. This is the fully stretched position of the pectoral muscles. From the stretched position, move both elbows downward and across the torso. The elbows should almost touch as your forearms cross the midabdominal area. The majority of the pectorals' muscle fibers run parallel to this down-and-across movement.

The Nautilus double chest machine was designed according to the function of the pectoral muscles. This machine works the chest by providing resistance to the arms as they move down and across the torso. Training the chest from other "angles" is not necessary. In fact, it simply depletes your recovery ability.

If the Nautilus double chest machine is not available, the best barbell exercise for the pectoral muscles is the decline press performed with shoulder-width hand spacing. This exercises the pectoral muscles with a barbell in the closest-to-correct angle that is possible.

Thus, you should look for the exercise that will most closely simulate the primary function of the muscle mass you are working. Angle training is a step in the wrong direction. It is the quality of the exercise that is important, not the quantity.

NEGATIVE TRAINING

Q. *Is there anything wrong with performing negative-accentuated repetitions by moving up with two limbs, then down with the right, repeating this until the right limb is exhausted, then switching to the left limb—as opposed to alternating between the right and left limbs on every other repetition?*
A. There is nothing wrong with this style of negative-accentuated training. However, you should note this modification on your workout card.

Q. *Is performing negative workouts more than once a week a problem?*
A. Yes. The problem centers around the fact that negative workouts, compared to normal positive-negative workouts, make greater demands on your recovery ability. A heavy negative workout often requires 72 hours or more for the body to overcompensate and get stronger. This is why it is a good idea to train in a negative fashion only once a week. If a Monday-Wednesday-Friday workout schedule is used, the negative routine would be performed on Friday.

Q. *Does Nautilus recommend standing on the weight stacks as a means of providing additional negative exercise?*
A. Both standing on the weight stacks and applying hand resistance to the weight stacks are haphazard ways to train in a negative fashion. This is occasionally done under very controlled conditions at the Nautilus headquarters in Florida. The problem is that it is very difficult to record what you have done after you have finished such a set. How much pressure was applied by the assistant's hand or foot? Was it applied equally throughout the entire range of movement? Such negative training is guesswork at best.

FORCED REPETITIONS

Q. *What about forced repetitions on Nautilus equipment?*

A. When you reach momentary muscular failure on the positive portion of an exercise, you usually terminate the set. However, if an assistant helps you by pushing or pulling on the movement arm, you can successfully lower the resistance negatively for several more repetitions. Such assistance has been called *forced repetition*.

Forced repetitions allow you to exhaust your negative strength, as well as positive strength on a given exercise. Initially, if you have never tried forced repetitions, the technique will produce very good results. This is probably due not only to the negative exhaustion factor, but to the shock to your system as well.

Most bodybuilders, however, carry a good thing too far. They start applying forced repetitions during each set of every workout, which probably means they are overtraining. Or, in their haste to get to the forced repetitions, they fail to work to muscular exhaustion on the initial positive movements, which usually leads to a gradual reduction in the intensity of the exercise.

If you know that you are going to be subjected to forced repetitions at the end of a normal set, you usually fail to produce a 100% effort during the normal repetitions. You will stop one or two movements short of an all-out effort in preparation for an optimum display of strength during the following forced repetitions.

In either situation, it soon becomes very difficult to record briefly and accurately on a workout card what has been accomplished.

The full benefit of forced repetitions occurs when your training partner only *occasionally* applies this technique, perhaps once every two weeks. Even then, you should not be aware that you are going to do forced repetitions until you have completed your last possible normal repetition. Do not underestimate the element of surprise in the application of forced repetitions.

REST BETWEEN MACHINES

Q. *How long should a bodybuilder rest between Nautilus machines?*

A. There is no advantage in resting longer than 15 to 20 seconds. In fact, there are several good reasons why rest periods should be brief. First, by moving quickly from one machine to the next, you are able to sustain a pulse rate that stimulates improved heart and lung endurance. Second, keeping a high pulse rate will make a lighter-than-normal weight feel heavier; thus, the exercise is equally effective but safer. Third, the overall workout is much more efficient. Why take 40 minutes to perform a workout when it could be performed in only 20 minutes?

ENDURANCE AND FLEXIBILITY

Q. *Are there benefits other than building muscular size and strength in using Nautilus equipment?*

A. Yes. A trainee who exercises properly on Nautilus equipment can most definitely improve his heart and lung endurance and joint flexibility, as well as muscular size and strength.

The important factors to remember about Nautilus exercise designed to improve heart and lung endurance follow:

1. The exercise must be hard enough to elevate the pulse rate to 70–85% of its maximum rate, which is usually about 150 beats per minute.

2. This rate must be sustained for a minimum of 10 minutes.

3. Such exercise must be repeated at least three times a week.

For flexibility the limbs must be stretched into positions that extend far beyond the normal range of movement. It takes heavy resistance to produce such a degree of stretching. This stretching is provided in the negative portion of all single-joint rotary movements performed on Nautilus machines.

High levels of heart and lung endurance, joint flexibility,

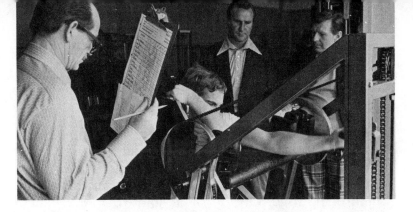

Arthur Jones supervises the high-intensity training of a cadet at the U. S. Military Academy. Observing are coach Don Shula of the Miami Dolphins and Dr. Robert Nirschl. It took Jones twenty years to learn that *two sets* of an exercise are better than four sets and ten more years to learn that *one set* is better than two. (Photo by Inge Cook)

and muscular size and strength also provide valuable protection against injury to any athlete. An extensive research program was conducted at the U.S. Military Academy, West Point, New York, in April and May of 1975. Twenty varsity athletes were trained for six weeks by two Nautilus experts. In only 17 workouts averaging less than 30 minutes each, these athletes increased their strength an average of 59%. They also improved their heart and lung endurance so much that they reduced their average time for the two-mile run by 88 seconds. They increased their flexibility from 10 to 20 times as much as the control group of other athletes who were trained in the traditional manner.

The Nautilus group suffered no injuries. Several of them started the program with previously damaged hamstring muscles and finished with no trace of the old injuries. Not only did they recover from their previous trouble, but they greatly increased the strength of their hamstrings and other major muscle groups.

The Nautilus-trained athletes performed only one set of each of approximately 12 exercises in every workout, and their speed of movement was fairly slow. Yet their average level of improvement was several hundred percent better than any results ever shown by any other research program. Such a level of improvement had always been considered impossible, and it is impossible except with Nautilus.

PARTIAL REPETITIONS

Q. *On a Nautilus machine, if you cannot complete a full range of movement after about eight repetitions, should you continue to do partial repetitions until failure?*

A. The answer to this question depends on the Nautilus machine being used. On the single-joint rotary movements, such as the pullover, leg extension, and leg curl, the cams are about 90% efficient at working the desired muscle. Partial repetitions should *not* be done on the single-joint machines. Doing so puts disproportionate emphasis on part of the movement, since the cam is designed to work the muscle proportionally.

With the multiple-joint exercises, such as the leg press, overhead press, and pulldown, partial repetitions at the end of a set may be advantageous. Multiple-joint exercises on Nautilus machines are about 25% efficient. It is impossible to attain a proper full-range strength curve on such a movement, so partial repetitions may be called for.

NAUTILUS DOUBLE MACHINES

Q. *Is it important for a bodybuilder to use the Nautilus double machines during each workout?*

A. All Nautilus double machines—compound leg, pullover/torso arm, behind neck/torso arm, double chest, and double shoulder—were designed to make use of the pre-exhaustion technique. The purpose of the pre-exhaustion technique is to pre-exhaust a body part by performing a single-joint exercise that isolates specific muscles. This is immediately followed by a multiple-joint exercise that brings into action other surrounding muscles to force the pre-exhausted muscle to work even harder.

Using the pre-exhaustion technique on the five Nautilus double machines in a single workout makes enormous demands on your recovery ability. Such a demanding workout should be performed no more than once a week. Two or three of the double machines, but not all five, may be used during every workout.

39

more questions and answers

GETTING LEAN

Q. *What is the best way to become lean for a physique contest?*

A. To become lean, you must reduce your subcutaneous fat as much as possible. Genetics, calories, and nutritional balance are the key factors in reducing subcutaneous fat.

First, you must be blessed with favorable genetics (see Chapter 17). Second, even with favorable genetics on your side, your caloric output must exceed your caloric input. Finally, to make certain that a reduced caloric diet actually produces fat loss, rather than muscle loss, the diet must be balanced among the basic four food groups. A balanced diet is composed of several small servings a day of these groups: meat, dairy products, fruits and vegetables, and breads and cereals.

Remember that there is no quick and easy way to reduce subcutaneous fat. It takes discipline and patience.

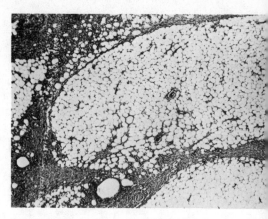

The average bodybuilder has billions of fat cells throughout his body. Examined under a microscope, the cells resemble a bubble bath. A trainee can *not* destroy fat cells. He can only shrink them through a program of proper diet and exercise. (Photo by Nellie Wiggins)

SWEATING AND FAT

Q. *Will sweating in a steam or sauna bath help reduce fat?*

A. No, absolutely not! There is no fat in sweat. In fact, as dehydration occurs through sweating, the body actually *conserves* its fat stores.

Q. *What about wearing a rubber belt around the midsection to get rid of fat?*

A. Again, this is a self-destructive step. Sweating simply dehydrates the body's tissues. And since more than 70% of a bodybuilder's muscles are composed of water, a considerable amount of the water lost in profuse sweating comes from the muscles.

You will always get better results if you train in cool, well-ventilated areas and drink plenty of water. It is almost impossible for a bodybuilder to drink too much water.

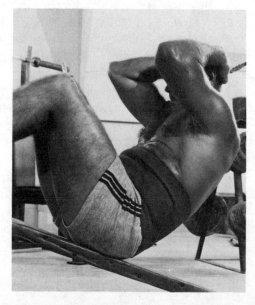

This photograph illustrates two popular myths that are frequently adopted by bodybuilders: one, the belief that sit-ups are effective for removing fat from the waist; two, the belief that you can sweat fat off by wearing a rubber belt.

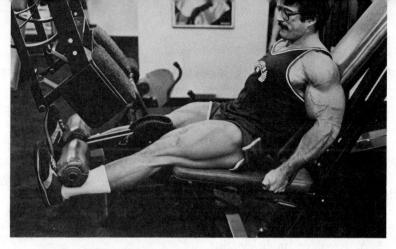

Mr. Universe, Mike Mentzer, knows the importance of brief, high-intensity exercise combined with adequate rest and recovery. (Photo by Ellington Darden)

MUSCULAR GROWTH

Q. *Is there a simple way to explain how a muscle grows?*

A. Muscular growth is a result of what physiologists call overcompensation. At least this is true in regard to growth that exceeds normal development. Arthur Jones often cites the formation of a callus as an example of this overcompensation process. The skin on your palms is naturally thicker than it is on the backs of your hands. This extra thickness will be found on the palms even if you never perform any of the hard work that is required. But if you perform hard work with your hands, work that brings your hands into contact with abrasive objects, the thickness of the skin on your palms may not be sufficient to protect you. In this case you will develop a callus in any area exposed to such work, *as long as the conditions are right.*

For the conditions to be right, the work must be hard enough to stimulate the growth of a callus. Second, the work must not reach an amount that will *prevent* the growth of a callus. If you work hard, the growth of a callus will be stimulated. If you work too much, the growth will not take place.

No amount of gentle rubbing on the palm of your hand will stimulate the growth of a callus. It is not the amount of contact that causes a callus to grow. Instead, if you rub your hand only once, but hard, the growth of a callus will be stimulated.

If you rub your hand too many times, or too often, however, no callus will result. The body may be trying to form a callus, but the rubbing will remove the growing tissue faster than the body can provide it.

To summarize:

1. Your palm has no callus.

2. You rub the palm gently with your finger repeatedly and often.

3. No callus will ever result because no extra skin is required to protect your hand from such contact. The normal thickness of the skin is adequate under these circumstances.

4. Then, you rub the palm once with a file—hard. And you repeat this action once each 48 hours.

5. A callus will start to form immediately, and it will quickly grow to a great thickness.

6. Since the normal thickness of the skin cannot provide adequate protection under these conditions, extra protection is required. The body will provide this extra protection in the form of a callus.

7. This is *overcompensation*. The body replaces the normal thickness of skin that was reduced by the pressure of the file and then overcompensates by adding extra tissue in the form of the callus.

8. If the conditions are exactly right, the growth of the callus will be very rapid and it will continue until the hands are protected by a layer of tissue as thick and as hard as some shoe soles. But if you rub the file on your palm too much or too often, no callus will ever result. You will remove the extra tissue as fast as the body provides it.

Muscular growth takes place in a similar fashion for similar reasons. Part of such growth is natural. But beyond a certain point muscular growth must be stimulated. Such extra growth will not occur unless it is stimulated by heavy demands on the existing levels of muscular size resulting from natural growth. And it cannot occur unless the recovery ability of the system is able to compensate and overcompensate at the same time.

If all the recovery ability of the system is used up in efforts to compensate, no energy will be left for the overcompensation that produces greater-than-normal growth.

In practice, most bodybuilders fall into a pattern in which the amount of their training uses up all of their recovery ability. Growth thus becomes impossible. Second, they seldom train hard enough to stimulate overcompensation, so little or no growth can occur even though their system is capable of overcompensation.

ARM TRAINING

Q. *In some of the routines listed in Chapter 37, no specific exercises were listed for the upper arms. Why?*

A. To work all the major muscle groups in each workout, you would have to perform more than 20 different exercises. If you performed 20 or more exercises properly, in a high-intensity fashion, you would soon be overtrained. Your progress would stop altogether or gradually decline.

Fortunately, because of the indirect effect, you do not need to exercise every major muscle group each time you train. That is why it is not necessary to concentrate on the smaller muscle groups, such as the upper arms, forearms, calves, and neck, during every workout. Furthermore, working the smaller muscle groups intensely once a week often produces better results than training them two or three times a week.

ADVANCED BODYBUILDING

Q. *Should advanced bodybuilders perform more than 12 exercises during a workout?*

A. No! Rather than perform more exercises, advanced bodybuilders should perform fewer exercises than should a

Advanced bodybuilders such as Joe Means should actually perform fewer exercises in a workout than a beginner.

beginning bodybuilder. *Recovery ability* is the primary reason for this fact.

Your recovery ability does not increase in proportion to your ability to get stronger. For example, some physiologists say that a typical, untrained man has the potential to increase his strength approximately 300%. But he can only increase his recovery ability about 50%.

It is important to remember that the stronger and more advanced you become, the fewer exercises you need.

Q. *How do you know when to do fewer exercises?*
A. The most reliable way to know when to do fewer exercises is to examine your workout chart carefully. In six months, you should be able to double your strength in all major exercises. Progress on the Nautilus leg extension machine is offered as an example, but other machines would apply equally well.

If, on January 1, you perform 60 pounds for 10 repetitions on the leg extension machine, then, by July 1, if you have trained properly, you should be able to perform 120 pounds for 10 repetitions. Since the leg extension works the quadriceps muscles, your quadriceps are twice as strong.

After you have doubled your strength, your total number of exercises should be reduced from 12 to 10, and your high-intensity workouts per week reduced from three to two. You should continue to train three times a week, but only two of these workouts are to be of high intensity. You would train hard on Mondays and Fridays and moderately on Wednesdays. The Wednesday workout consists of the same exercises and resistance as the hard workout, but the exercise is ended two or three repetitions sooner. The medium workout does not stimulate growth, but it does prevent strength loss. It does not use up as much of your recovery ability as a hard workout.

In another six months, you should be expected to triple your strength or to progress on the leg extension from 120 pounds to 180 pounds. But to quadruple your strength, or progress from 180 to 240 pounds, another reduction is in order. Instead of 10 exercises, you now perform only 8 exercises. In place of two hard training days a week, you have one. You still train three times a week, but only one session is at high intensity. The other two are of medium intensity, as you stop each set several repetitions short of an all-out effort.

Thus, in 18 months, or 24 months at most, the average bodybuilder—if he has trained properly—can expect to reach his full genetic potential. But, in order to accomplish this goal in two years, as opposed to 10 years, *he must train less as he gets stronger*—and he must keep accurate records of all his workouts.

ONE SET VS. MULTIPLE SETS

Q. *Why is one set of an exercise better than two or more sets?*

A. The answer to this question is based on two factors: You must *stimulate* growth, but you must also *permit* growth to occur. Stimulation occurs best as a result of high-intensity exercise. As the intensity of the exercise increases, greater demands are placed on your recovery ability. The stimulation of a muscle is most effective when it is as brief as possible.

Thus, if you can stimulate maximum growth from one set, which you can, a second set merely uses up some of your valuable recovery ability. As a result, muscular growth is not permitted. On the contrary, it is severely limited.

Arthur Jones uses the following analogy in reference to the performance of more than one set of an exercise: "It takes only one properly placed shot to kill a rabbit or an elephant. Additional shots will serve no purpose except unnecessary destruction of the meat. The same is true of exercise."

Q. *Didn't Casey Viator gain most of his muscular size and strength from performing multiple sets with barbells?*

The muscular physique of Casey Viator. (Photo by Inge Cook)

A. Casey did train several years on conventional equipment prior to meeting Arthur Jones in 1970. His best results, however, came during the several months that preceded the 1971 Mr. America contest. Arthur Jones personally supervised each of his workouts during this period.

The important thing to remember about Casey is that he had the genetic potential to be big and strong before he ever became interested in training. Almost any type of resistance exercise—gymnastics, barbells, Universal Gym, or Nautilus—would have given him results. He inherited extremely long muscle bellies. Actual measurements show that Casey has four times as much muscular mass potential as the average American male.

Arthur Jones makes it a point to tell bodybuilders who visit the Nautilus headquarters that Casey has a sister with similar potential who weighs a solid 180 pounds. And she has never done any resistance training.

Q. *All the bodybuilding greats perform multiple sets. What bodybuilding star has only performed one set of 12 exercises per workout?*

A. Dozens of well-known bodybuilders visited the Nautilus headquarters in Lake Helen, Florida, during the early 1970s. Each was put through a high-intensity workout on Nautilus equipment. Generally, the workout consisted of no more than one set of 12 exercises. The ones who made it through the entire workout, and some of them did not, felt a degree of stimulation and fatigue that they had not previously experienced. And all the ones who continued to train under Nautilus supervision for as short as a week noted a remarkably fast rate of muscular growth.

Brief high-intensity Nautilus training, however, is not fun. And it was never intended to be. High-intensity exercise is hard, brutally hard. Even though it is enormously productive, most bodybuilders who experience a proper Nautilus workout would rather return to their multiple-set, long, drawn-out, medium-intensity workouts. Once you are addicted to the much easier, multiple-set workouts, it is almost impossible to switch. But Nautilus does hope that it can direct the bodybuilders of the future toward a more logical and productive program.

ENJOYMENT OR RESULTS?

Q. *Isn't it possible that some bodybuilders simply enjoy training with barbells more than Nautilus?*

A. Yes, that is exactly the case. Even Arthur Jones, the inventor of the Nautilus machines, says there is a certain sense of completion that a trainee gets after each repetition with a barbell. Since there is little or no resistance in the fully-contracted position of most barbell exercises, the individual can rest briefly. Naturally, this brief resting position is enjoyable.

With Nautilus single-joint rotary machines, it is impossible to rest in the contracted position. Rather than being the easiest part of the exercise, it is the hardest part.

For training, barbells are much more enjoyable than Nautilus machines. But Nautilus is much more productive.

40

a step into the future

Teaching old dogs new tricks may not be impossible, but it is a difficult, thankless job at best. In the end, the eventual acceptance of new equipment and training systems will depend primarily on a new generation of bodybuilders— men who have not been so thoroughly brainwashed that they are literally afraid to learn.

The most productive training routines of the future will be built around equipment much like Nautilus machines that are already in wide use across the United States. The major improvement will be the incorporation of computer technology into Nautilus machines. Computerized Nautilus machines of the future will make exercise harder and briefer and thus more productive.

THE FUTURE NAUTILUS CENTER

You enter the Nautilus center of the future and identify yourself by punching your code number into the keyboard,

295

or miniterminal, on each machine. The machine will be promptly and automatically set for you by the computer with careful consideration given to such things as your existing strength, range of movement, age, and previous workout history. From that moment on, a monitor attached to the machine will tell you what to do, how to do it, how hard to do it, and how often to do it. And the computer will keep a permanent record of what is actually done. The level of resistance will be whatever you require at that point.

Computerized machines of the future will require you to perform each repetition in perfect style. When cheating occurs, you will instantly be informed. When you are doing the movement correctly, the machine will reinforce your actions.

Computerized machines will do many things that no human being can. They will preserve an exact record of your workouts. The computer will automatically and instantly change the workouts when that is appropriate. Sensing and reacting to any reasonable number of physiological factors, the machine will assure a degree of safety not previously possible.

Nautilus machines of the future can be computer programmed for almost any purpose. But perhaps of greatest importance is the fact that a machine will not lose interest in the trainees working under its supervision.

Adhering to proper form seems to be the most pressing problem in performing high-intensity exercise. There seems to be a natural tendency to permit a rapid deterioration in the style of performance and to reduce the intensity of exercise without being aware of it. However, if proper form is maintained, and if the intensity of work is correct, then Nautilus-assisted exercise can produce gratifying results in a short time.

Poor form and lowered intensity result from a desire to demonstrate progress. Under the mistaken impression that they can improve at a faster rate, many bodybuilders change the form or intensity of an exercise. And they are encouraged by the fact that doing so increases the amount of resistance they can handle. But when that happens they are throwing the weight, not lifting it.

An increase in resistance is meaningless unless the form remains unchanged, and no amount of exercise will produce results if the form is not good. Future computerized Nautilus equipment will take this and similar errors out of training.

When will the computerized machines be available to the public? Nautilus has been building and testing them for more than five years. Millions of dollars worth of prototypes have been built, tested, redesigned, and rebuilt. Arthur Jones is a perfectionist. He must be satisfied that his machines are not only high in quality but easy to operate and basically foolproof. The 1982 prototypes come very close to meeting the required standards. One of the few remaining tests is a large-scale program that will involve various strength curves, speeds of movement, and repetitions. Nautilus hopes that the computerized machines will be fully tested and on the market in 1983.

HARDER-SLOWER-BRIEFER

Data collected so far on the new machines reinforce existing Nautilus training principles. The computerized machines make stricter exercise possible. Stricter exercise allows a muscle group to be better isolated. Better muscle isolation in turn means harder overall exercise for each part of the body. And the harder the exercise, the briefer it must be. Recent computer testing indicates that the intensity may be so great on some machines—for example, the biceps curl— that the repetitions may have to be reduced to only five or six for maximum muscular stimulation. More repetitions than six, it is anticipated, may make demands on the body's recovery ability that are greater than it can handle.

The computerized Nautilus machines seem destined to verify what Arthur Jones experienced more than 20 years ago and has been advocating vigorously for the last 10:

"Don't look for ways to make exercise easier, faster, and longer. Look for ways to make it harder, slower, and briefer."

In the future, the most efficient and productive system of bodybuilding will surely be based on the Nautilus philosophy. This philosophy can be summarized in three simple but rigid rules:

Train *harder.*
Train *slower.*
Train *briefer.*

bibliography

Barrett, Stephen (editor). *The Health Robbers*. Philadelphia: George F. Stickley, Publishers, 1980.

Beller, Anne Scott. *Fat and Thin*. New York: Farrar, Straus and Giroux, 1977.

Darden, Ellington. *The Nautilus Book: An Illustrated Guide to Physical Fitness the Nautilus Way*. Chicago: Contemporary Books, Inc., 1980.

Darden, Ellington. *The Nautilus Nutrition Book*. Chicago: Contemporary Books, Inc., 1981.

Goldberg, Alfred L., and others. "Mechanism of Work-Induced Hypertrophy of Skeletal Muscle." *Medicine and Science in Sports* 7: 248–261, 1975.

Gowitzke, Barbara A., and Milner, Morris. *Understanding the Scientific Basis of Human Movement*. Baltimore: Williams & Wilkins, 1980.

Huxley, H. E. "The Mechanism of Muscular Contraction." *Scientific American* 213: 18–27, December 1965.

Jones, Arthur. *Nautilus Training Principles, Bulletin No. 1.* DeLand, Florida: Nautilus Sports/Medical Industries, 1970.

———. "The Upper Body Squat." *Iron Man* 29, 5: 41, 47, 71, June 1970.

———. "Total Omni-Directional, Direct Exercise System." *Iron Man* 29, 6: 30, 31, 73, 74, September 1970.

———. "A Totally New Concept in Exercise and Equipment." *Iron Man* 30, 1: 28, 29, 57, 58, 62–66, October 1970.

———. *Nautilus Training Principles, Bulletin No. 2.* DeLand, Florida: Nautilus Sports/Medical Industries, 1971.

———. "Accentuate the Negative." *Iron Man* 32, 2: 30, 31, 56–59, January 1973.

———. "The Colorado Experiment." *Iron Man* 32, 6: 34–37, August 1973.

Kendall, H. O.; Kendall, F. P.; and Wadsworth, G. E. *Muscles: Testing and Function.* Baltimore: Williams & Wilkins, 1971.

Komi, P. V., and Buskirk, E. R. "Effect of Eccentric and Concentric Muscle Conditioning on Tension and Electrical Activity of Human Muscle." *Ergonomics* 15: 417–434, 1972.

Langley, L. L.; Telford, I. R.; and Christensen, J. B. *Dynamic Anatomy and Physiology.* New York: McGraw-Hill, 1974.

Peterson, James A. (editor). *Total Fitness: The Nautilus Way.* West Point, New York: Leisure Press, 1978.

Rasch, Philip J., and Burke, Roger K. *Kinesiology and Applied Anatomy.* Philadelphia: Lea & Febiger, 1978.

Ryan, Allan J. "Anabolic Steroids Are Fool's Gold." Paper presented at the 64th Annual Meeting, Federation of American Societies for Experimental Biology, American Society for Pharmacology and Experimental Therapeutics, April 15, 1980.

index